Great Lakes Ore Docks and Ore Cars

Patrick C. Dorin

Iconografix

Iconografix
PO Box 446
Hudson, Wisconsin 54016 USA

Library of Congress Control Number: 2007932530

ISBN-13: 978-1-58388-202-3
ISBN-10: 1-58388-202-2

07 08 09 10 11 12 6 5 4 3 2 1

Printed in China

Cover and book design by Dan Perry

Copyedited by Andy Lindberg

TABLE OF CONTENTS

ACKNOWLEDGMENTS

Not a single book could ever be completed without the assistance of knowledge levels of many people. The following people provided a substantial amount of data for this book on ore docks and cars including many photographs and drawings:

Patricia Maus of the Northeast Minnesota Historical Center – University of Minnesota-Duluth; Tim Schandel of the Lake Superior Railroad Museum; Superior Views, Marquette, Michigan; Doug Buell; Joe Piersen of the C&NW Historical Society; Dan Mackey; William Raia; Thomas Dorin; Michael Dorin; Steve Ruce; Gordon Jomini; Staffan Ehnbom; Robert C. Anderson; Robert Blomquist; and Gary Wildung. The author also wishes to thank his wife Karen for her review of the writing, and her patience with not only this book project, but also dozens of others.

Finally, a thank you to Dylan Frautschi and other staff at Iconografix for the time and work with the layout and the many steps toward publication.

Should anyone's name have been inadvertently not listed with the above, the writer trusts it will be found in the appropriate place within the book.

Thank you each and everyone for your time, patience, wisdom and friendship in the research and gathering of materials.

PROLOGUE

The iron mining industry is quite extensive throughout the area known as the Lake Superior Iron Ore District, which includes Michigan, Wisconsin, Minnesota and Ontario. There were and are other prominent iron mining regions to the northeast and east of Lake Superior in Ontario as well Quebec and Labrador. All of the iron ore was and is transported by rail to a wide number of lake ports on Lake Superior, Lake Michigan and Lake Huron.

The major U.S. iron ranges included the Mesabi, Vermilion, and Cuyuna in northern Minnesota, and the Spring Valley in southeastern Minnesota. The Marquette and Menominee Ranges are located in Michigan, while the Gogebic Range extends from east of Wakefield, Michigan, to west of Mellen, Wisconsin. Wisconsin played host to three other mining regions in the central sections of the state which included the Black River Falls, Baraboo and the Mayville Districts.

Canada also has an extensive listing of mining areas. North and west of Thunder Bay (once known as two cities, Fort William and Port Arthur), there were five areas.

The closest to Thunder Bay was the Matawin District. Just a bit west of that area is the Gunflint Range, which actually extends into northern Minnesota. Going west along the Canadian National Railway main line one comes to the Atikokan District and the Steep Rock Range near Atikokan, Ontario. To the far northwest of Thunder Bay, well over 200 miles, is the Bruce Lake Area. Moving to the east side of Lake Superior one can find the Michipicoten District, the Goulais District and the Moose Mountain District.

There is always something new to learn and know about any subject, and when it is about railroads, shall we say, "The sky is the limit." This book lists all of the ore docks constructed on Lakes Superior and Michigan, as well as their operational life span right up to the present time in late 2006. Each chapter for each railroad includes the types of ore docks once or currently operated, as well as a roster of ore cars from the 1940s to the present time, photos of the ore docks and ore cars, and pertinent data. It is hoped that this book provides some new perspectives for historical and future logistics, and for the artwork of model railroading.

Happy Railroading,

Patrick C. Dorin
Superior, Wisconsin
November 1, 2006

INTRODUCTION
ORE DOCK TECHNOLOGY AND ORE CAR DESIGNS

The ore docks and ore cars in northern Minnesota, Wisconsin, Michigan and Ontario were truly artistic designs, and they provided a balanced transportation system for the movement of a wide variety of iron ores from the different iron ranges throughout the entire Lake Superior region. In many cases, the steel companies required a certain mixing of the ores for specific iron and steel production, and the mixing of ores could be done very effectively on the gravity type pocket ore docks. Such is not the case as we move deeper into the 21st century with the taconite pellets (and possibly iron nuggets in the near future) from the individual plants. In fact, as a side bar, there were once hundreds of mines throughout the area, but at this time (2006), there are only seven taconite or iron ore pellet plants operating in northern Michigan and Minnesota. However, there is a variety of pellet products – but that is different story.

Most of the ore docks in operation from the beginning of the twentieth century were gravity pocket type docks with chutes on 12-foot centers for loading into the ore carriers. This type of dock lent itself very nicely to the process of mixing ores for a particular shipment. The iron ore lines had some very interesting work to do. The ore cars were loaded at the different mines for a particular mix as ordered by the steel companies. There could be as many as a dozen types of ore to be mixed for a boat shipment. Therefore, the railroads had a great deal of classification work to do at the ore dock yards with the appropriate placement for dumping. Just one example is that a lump type of ore would be dumped in the pockets first with various types of fines following. In fact, even with iron ore and taconite pellets, these would sometimes be mixed with different types of natural iron ores. Interestingly enough, sometimes just a half of a carload would have to be dumped before the other types of ores followed. This required a great deal of switching and made some interesting railroad operations.

The gravity pocket type of dock was developed with 12-foot centers for each pocket so that the placement of the dumping chutes could match hatch placement on the ore boats. The ore cars were designed at the 24-foot long length, and thus fit over every other pocket for unloading into the ore dock. Each cut of cars shoved on to the dock had to be placed appropriately so that every pocket was loaded in anticipation of a scheduled boat arrival.

Other types of ore dock were (and are) conveyor belt systems with and without silo ore/pellet storage areas. Two such examples are the former Chicago and North Western Railway's newest ore dock at Escanaba,

Michigan, and the Burlington Northern (BNSF) dock No. 5 at Superior, Wisconsin. Still another type of dock were the bucket loaders.

There was a wide variety of steel ore cars operated for the iron ore traffic. The tonnage capacities for the 24-foot long cars ranged from 50 tons to the newer 70- and 75-ton capacity cars. The latest designs in the 1960s went up to the 85- and 90-ton capacities.

The Burlington Northern brought about a new ore car design 34 feet long and with a 100-ton capacity. This coincided with the new dumping and storage facility in Superior where the ore cars were no longer placed on the ore docks for unloading. This eventually led to the total elimination of the former BN, Great Northern and Northern Pacific 24-foot cars.

The Algoma Central Railway also had larger types of hopper cars for their ore hauling to Sault Ste. Marie, Ontario. The Bessemer and Lake Erie Railroad located in Ohio and Pennsylvania, although not a Lake Superior Region Ore Railroad, handled the Lake Superior area ores from their dock on Lake Erie. The B&LE had its own design of ore cars that were very similar to the Lake Superior design. They also had purchased a number of cars from the Duluth, Missabe and Iron Range Railway. The Chicago and North Western also purchased a number of the B&LE ore cars. Thus one could find a mix of cars throughout the region, not only for ore hauling, but also coal, stone, gravel and sand traffic. As a side note – it is interesting to know that ore cars were often used for coal deliveries to coal yards in many cities and towns throughout the entire mid-west.

Although there have been a number of changes in ore car design during the 25 years (1980 to 2006), one can still observe the 24-foot cars in operation in Minnesota and Michigan. The DM&IR, now part of the Canadian National, and the Lake Superior and Ishpeming Railroads still own a large fleet of the 24-foot cars for service to the ore docks in Duluth, Two Harbors and Marquette. The former C&NW ore cars – later to the Wisconsin Central which is now part of the CN, are also still in operation between the Marquette Range and Escanaba.

The following diagrams and photos illustrate the basic technology or design of the pocket type ore dock, as well as the differences between the various Lake Superior ore cars, or more specifically, the Minnesota and Michigan ore cars. The Michigan cars were narrower than the Minnesota cars and could fit on any ore dock at any port. However, the Minnesota cars could not fit side by side on the ore docks in Marquette and Escanaba.

The historical information for this photo from Superior Views in Marquette is missing. This illustration shows the types of ore docks built in the late 19th Century, which were in the 40 to 50 feet high category. There are two completed docks in this photo, with a third one to the right under construction. It almost appears that it could be Two Harbors, Minnesota. Note the breakwater in the background. *Date unknown, Superior Views / Viewsofthepast.com*

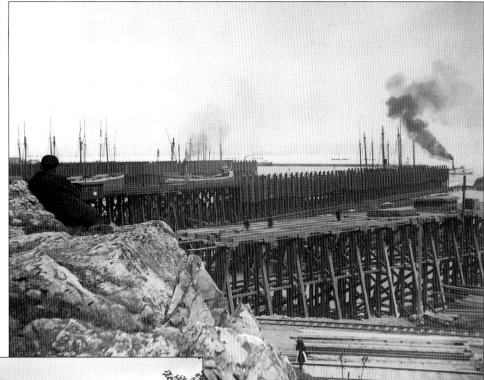

Most of the ore docks in the Lake Superior Region were high level facilities, generally 70 to 80 feet high. Approaches were built with bridge type construction to reach the higher levels. The tops of the docks had openings for the ore to be dumped from the ore cars and into pockets. The bottom of the pockets had a gate system to keep the ore in the pocket until the arrival of an ore boat for shipment. Upon arrival, dock operators would open the gate system which allowed the ore, and later iron ore or taconite pellets, to flow into the ship. This view of the Lake Superior and Ishpeming Railroad ore dock in Marquette, Michigan illustrates part of the approach and the chutes alongside the facility for ship loading. *Patrick C. Dorin*

This view of the dismantled Duluth, South Shore and Atlantic Railroad ore dock at Marquette shows the angle of the pockets as well as the connecting links for lowering the chutes into the lake vessels. The South Shore dock was dismantled leaving only the structure still standing in Lake Superior. *2003, Patrick C. Dorin*

This view of the Soo Line ore dock in Ashland illustrates part of the approach to the dock itself. The Soo Line ore dock, as the DSS&A dock in Marquette, was a concrete dock. Note the timber approach connecting with the final concrete section to the ore dock. *2003, Patrick C. Dorin*

The LS&I ore dock in Marquette is of concrete construction with a steel type of bridge approach. Also note the placement of the chutes, which are on 12-foot centers for each of the ore dock pockets. *2003, Patrick C. Dorin*

The Lake Superior Region ore cars, with the 24-foot length, fit over every other ore dock pocket, which are on 12-foot centers. Here is an example of the pocket entry areas to accommodate the 24-foot ore cars on the top of a steel or a concrete constructed ore dock. The cars must be spotted directly over the pocket for dumping. Note how the DM&IR mini-quad ore car No. 52610's hopper doors are over the pocket, while the car trucks are over the dividers and cover one pocket when coupled to the next ore car. The next car hopper doors are over the next pocket. Note the double hoses at the end of the ore car. One hose is for the air brake system, while the other hose handles the retainer brakes on the train as it moves down steep grades into either Two Harbors or Duluth. This photo was taken on the DM&IR's No. 2 ore dock in Two Harbors. *Patrick C. Dorin*

The first ore cars ever built were of wood construction. The couplers, trucks, and parts of the under frame were of steel construction. This ore car, No. 7013, was one of the first types of cars operated in northern Minnesota, such as the Duluth and Iron Range. One of these types of cars is on display at the Two Harbors Museum, which is the former Duluth, Missabe and Iron Range Railway office and depot. In fact, the building still serves as a station for the North Shore Scenic Railroad between Duluth and Two Harbors. *Northeast Minnesota Historical Center, University of Minnesota Duluth, File: S3742 Box 16, Folder 46*

Ore car development continued from the 1890s well into the 2000s with the newest type of ore cars on the Burlington Northern Santa Fe, which operate over the same Great Northern trackage shown in this photo. This GN train illustrates a mixture of wooden 50-ton capacity ore cars at the left, with steel 50-ton cars with side platforms. These side platforms were designed for ore punchers to stand on the side of the car for pushing the ore out of the cars into the ore dock pockets. This eliminated much of the situation of having to stand on top of the ore to push it into the dock. The reason for this type of unloading process was because of sticky and wet ores that did not immediately drop out of the car when the hopper doors were opened. *Lake Superior Railroad Museum*

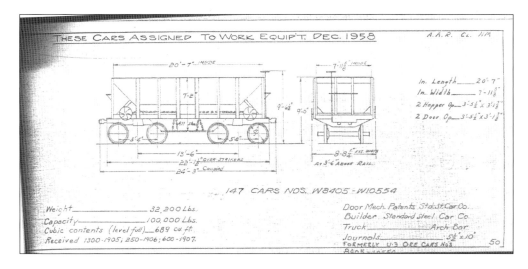

THESE CARS ASSIGNED TO WORK EQUIP'T. DEC. 1958

A.A.R. Cl. HM

In. Length _____ 20'-7"
In. Width _____ 7'-11⅜"
2 Hopper Op._ 3'-5½" X 3'-1⅜"
2 Door Op.___ 3'-5½" X 3'-1⅜"

147 CARS NOS. W8405 - W10554

Weight _____ 32,300 Lbs.
Capacity _____ 100,000 Lbs.
Cubic contents (level full) __ 689 cu.ft.
Received 1300 -1905; 250 -1906; 600 -1907.

Door Mech. Patents Std. St. Car Co.
Builder _ Standard Steel Car Co.
Truck _____ Arch Bar
Journals _____ 5½" x 10"
FORMERLY U.3 ORE CARS NOS.
8405 - 10554

The ore car length over couplers boiled down to a 24-foot length. However, there were some variations. The type of equipment illustrated in this diagram is a rib side, 50-ton capacity steel ore car. This group of cars was common on the Duluth, Missabe and Iron Range Railway, the Lake Superior and Ishpeming, and the Duluth, South Shore and Atlantic Railroad. This group for the DM&IR was built in between 1905 and 1907, and was assigned to work car service for rock and ballast in 1958. The cars were still in operation well into the 1960s and beyond to the 21st Century. *DM&IR Diagram*

This early 50-ton capacity steel ore car was photographed in ballast service on the Lake Superior and Mississippi Railroad, a tourist railroad alongside the St. Louis River on the western end of Duluth. This car matches the DM&IR diagram from the 8405 to 10554 series previously illustrated. Note the placement and type of side ribs as shown on the diagram. *1980s, Patrick C. Dorin*

This is a former DM&IR 50-ton ore car but with a different rib side arrangement. The lettering and numbers are all but gone. *Patrick C. Dorin*

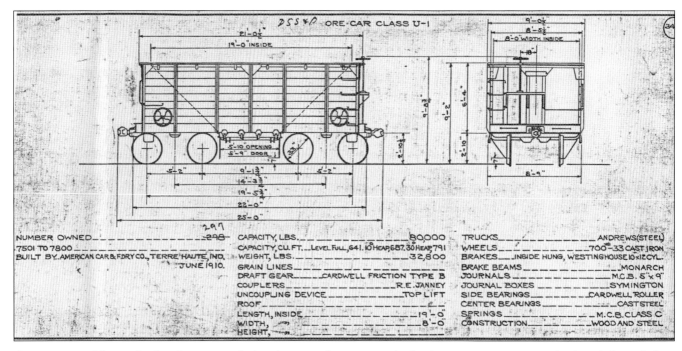

The construction of this wood and steel ore car goes back to the 1900s. This is an example of a Class U-1 40-ton capacity car for the Duluth, South Shore and Atlantic Railway, The car was 25 feet long over the couplers. Apparently the cars may have still been in service through 1927 and 1930 as the bottom of the diagram listed revisions during those years. *DSS&A Diagram*

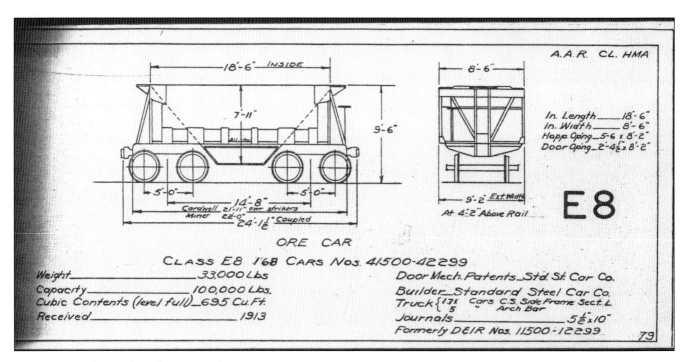

It would be nice to have a photo of every type of ore car ever constructed, but such did not happen. Jumping ahead to 1913, here is an example of slanted end ore cars originally built for the Duluth and Iron Range. The cars were still in ore service in the 1950s. *DM&IR Diagram*

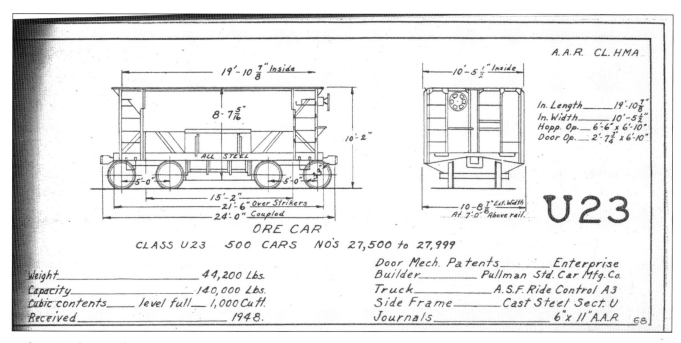

ORE CAR
CLASS U23   500 CARS   NO'S 27,500 to 27,999

By the 1920s, the 70- and 75-ton capacity ore cars had been designed and were being built for railroads such as the Duluth, Missabe and Northern and the Great Northern. This diagram illustrates a type of car that became quite prominent for both the DM&N, later the DM&IR, and the Great Northern. This type of ore car became a basic design for ore cars on the Great Northern, Soo Line, Northern Pacific, and the Canadian National. The CN became the newest ore line during the mid-1940s. This basic design could be called the "Minnesota Ore Cars" of the Lake Superior Ore Cars, and were somewhat wider than equipment in Michigan, which could be called the "Michigan Ore Cars." Both had capacities of 70 to 75 tons. *DM&IR Diagram*

As a sidebar for the ore cars: Ore cars in Minnesota were called "Jennies," while the cars in Michigan were referred to as "Jims."

CHAPTER 1

DULUTH, MISSABE & IRON RANGE RAILWAY

The Duluth, Missabe & Iron Range Railway has been (and is) the heaviest iron ore carrier in North America, and probably the world, for over a century. The railroad's history dates back to the 1880s and '90s with the birth of the Duluth and Iron Range Railway and the Duluth, Missabe and Northern Railway built north out of Two Harbors and Duluth respectively. By 1938 the two railroads had been merged into the single carrier. The DM&IR System has operated the largest number of ore docks of any railroad. In fact, altogether the two previous companies built a total of ten ore docks. The railroad also owned the largest fleet of ore cars, which is still the case as we move forward into the 21st Century. The Canadian National Railway purchased the DM&IR, as well as the sister railroad, the Bessemer and Lake Erie, in 2004. As we move through 2006, operations continue with the ore haulage. The future of iron ore pellets and shipping is in place for many decades into the 21st Century, and it will be interesting to see the changes in rail ore transportation and shipping on the Great Lakes.

The DM&IR Ore Dock Systems

The DM&IR operated ore docks in both Duluth and Two Harbors, Minnesota, which happen to be only about 30 miles from each other. Part of the first ore shipping that began in the Twin Ports of Duluth/Superior actually began with ore moving over the Duluth and Winnipeg Railroad ore dock in Superior. More about that ore dock in the chapter on the Great Northern Railway. The first ore dock for the D&IR/DM&N systems was built in Two Harbors. Let's take a look at the two ports with a brief history of the ore dock systems.

Two Harbors

The port of Two Harbors had a total of six ore docks. It was the largest number of ore docks at any port on the Great Lakes, although it did not have the greatest capacity. The docks were built as follows:

Dock No. 1

Construction of the No. 1 ore dock began about 1884, but it was not the first ore dock to be completed in Two Harbors. It was completed in 1885 and later rebuilt in the late 1890s. Eventually, the No. 1 wooden ore dock was replaced by a new steel ore dock in 1911 because of deterioration and its low level.

The new No. 1 dock was built with 224 pockets with a 56,000-ton capacity. The dock is 75 feet high and 1,344

feet long. The dock is in full operation in 2006.

Dock No. 2

The No. 2 wooden ore dock was completed ahead of the No. 1, which experienced several construction problems. The No. 2 was only 40 high with 46 pockets and 644 feet long from shore to the end of the dock. The original No. 2 was in operation from 1884 to 1910.

A new steel No. 2 ore dock was built in 1916 with 228 pockets and a capacity of 68,400 tons. All of the newer ore docks were built with pockets and loading systems on both sides on 12-foot centers. Thus the No. 2 had 114 pockets on each side with a length of 1,368 feet, pocket-to-pocket length. The No. 2 steel ore dock is still in full operation in 2006.

Dock No. 3

Wooden dock No. 3 was built in 1893, and extended in 1904–05. This dock contained 90 pockets.

Dock No. 4

This dock was constructed in 1892–93 and extended in 1902 to 168 pockets in length.

Dock No. 5

The last wooden ore dock to be constructed at Two Harbors was the No. 5. Built in 1895, the dock contained 168 pockets and was 54 feet, 6 inches high.

All of the wooden ore docks were at a relatively low level, such as described above between 40 and 55 feet in height. As the ore carriers became larger, it was more difficult to load the boats to capacity. This led to a new era in ore dock construction.

Dock No. 6

The No. 6 ore dock was the first steel ore dock to be constructed. It was 888 feet long and 75 feet high. The dock contained 148 pockets with a capacity of 44,000 tons.

The success of the No. 6 ore dock led to the construction of new No. 1 and 2 with the same basic design.

At the present time, the No. 6 is not in operation but is still standing. If necessary in the future, the dock could be connected to the taconite storage areas with a conveyor belt system. With some additional modifications, the dock could be used to load the 1,000-foot ore carriers on the Great Lakes.

Duluth

The Duluth, Missabe and Northern Railway built a grand total of six ore docks on Lake Superior in the West End of Duluth. The ore docks have been a primary asset for ore shipping since 1893. The ore dock construction era continued from 1893 until 1918 when the No. 6 ore dock was completed. The historical background of the six ore docks is as follows:

Dock No. 1

The very first DM&N dock was 2,300 feet long with a capacity of 57,600 tons. The dock was constructed with 384 pockets, each with a capacity of 150 tons. The first dock was 52 feet, 8 inches above the water, which eventually was too low. The dock was taken out of service in 1905.

Dock No. 2

The second ore dock was built during the time period 1895–96. It was rebuilt in 1905 when the first dock was taken out of service.

Dock No. 3

The third dock construction period took place during the years 1899 and 1900. The dock contained 192 pockets. Its first boatload was shipped on September 22, 1900.

The three ore docks had a combined storage capacity of 167,040 tons in 1901. However, a greater capacity would soon be required to accommodate the growth in iron ore shipping over the DM&N. In 1904, work began on an extension of the No. 3 ore dock with completion in 1905.

Dock No. 4

No. 4 was constructed in 1906 with 384 pockets with a capacity of 76,800 tons, which meant 200 tons per pocket. The new ore dock was 2,304 feet long, pocket-to-pocket length. At this point in time, the No. 4 ore dock was the largest timber ore dock ever constructed. It would also turn out to be the last wooden dock for either the D&IR or the DM&N. But it would not be the last ore dock to be constructed.

Dock No. 5

The next ore dock would be constructed of steel 80 feet high, 2,304 feet long with a storage capacity of 115,200 tons. The DM&N had built another record size ore dock during the time period 1913 and 1914. The original No. 1 and 2 ore docks were dismantled. The No. 3 and 4 would remain for a period of time.

Dock No. 6

Dock No. 6 was built during the time period 1917 and '18. Again we have a 2,304-foot long ore dock, pocket-to-pocket length, but this time with a record size of 153,600-ton storage capacity. It was the largest ore dock ever constructed in the world, and is still in operation today. In 1964, a ground storage area was placed in operation for taconite pellets with a capacity of 2.24 million tons. The No. 6 dock has 64 modified pockets for loading 1,000-foot ore carriers.

The following photographs and charts illustrate the DM&IR ore docks in Duluth and Two Harbors. For a period of time, the DM&N did operate four ore docks in Duluth, but No. 3 and 4 were eventually dismantled leaving the No. 6 dock to the left and No. 5 to the right when viewing the lake front from shore.

At the present time (2006), the DM&IR (now CN) operates three ore docks, the No. 1 and 2 at Two Harbors, and the No. 6 at Duluth. Ever since the late 1960s, the DM&IR was and is the only railroad serving two ports. (In fact, looking at it from the CN perspective since the company now owns the DM&IR and the Wisconsin Central, the CN serves three ports including Escanaba.) The 24-foot type ore cars are still the main segment of ore hauling for the DM&IR to both Duluth and Two Harbors. The next section of this chapter reviews the steel ore car fleet of the railroad through to the present system of operations in 2006.

DM&IR ORE CARS

The DM&IR ore car fleet served the iron ore and steel industry for well over 100 years, and as this is being written in 2006; many of the 24-foot steel ore cars built in the 1950s are still in reliable service. The DM&IR had a high level of maintenance for the equipment, which extended the life span of the equipment.

The ore cars were painted in a dark brown color with white lettering. This was the case with the Duluth, Missabe and Northern; which merged with the Duluth and Iron Range during the 1930s to become the Duluth, Missabe and Iron Range Railway.

When the DM&IR began rebuilding ore cars in the 1960s for taconite pellet service, the cars came out with a maroon scheme with yellow lettering. This scheme remained as the appropriate paint and lettering scheme for several decades. Furthermore, the DM&IR rebuilt a fleet of ore cars for ballast service, and they were painted yellow with maroon lettering. The DM&IR insignia was the center of the car sides.

As time went on, however, the cars did not receive the full paint scheme but simply DMIR lettering on the sides of the cars. In fact, this was simply painted over the insignia.

This was the case for equipment with the extensions as well as the fleet without the extensions.

A small number of the DM&IR ballast cars were sold to the Elgin, Joliet and Eastern Railway. On the "J," the cars retained their yellow color scheme with the EJ&E reporting marks in the center of the car. The EJ&E was once a sister railroad to the DM&IR with the U.S. Steel ownership. As of 2004, the Canadian National purchased the DM&IR. However, the ore cars are still operating with the DM&IR schemes as we move through 2006. The DM&IR ore car fleet, with the Missabe crews and many others, has done much to enrich the steel industry and the economy of North America.

The DM&IR Ore Car Roster

The DM&IR operated an ore car fleet with a great deal of variety, especially since the railroad was the result of the combination of the Duluth and Iron Range Railway and the Duluth, Missabe & Northern Railway. The following rosters illustrate the types of equipment in operation from the 1950s through 2004 and the CN takeover. The Lake Superior ore cars were (and are) 24 feet long, coupled length. However, the cars did have a variety of different lengths over strikers, heights and widths as listed below.

Note: Symbols LOS - Length Over Strikers, W - extreme width, and H - height

The 50-ton Ore Car Fleet

Number Series	Class	Remarks
8405 to 10554	U3	Tapered side car with rib sides LOS: 22'-1 1/2", W: 8'-8 1/4", H: 9'-6 1/2" Built 1905 to 1907, Standard Steel Car Company
100 to 849	U4	Tapered side car with rib sides
10555 to 11704	U4	Tapered side car with rib sides LOS: 22'-1", W: 8'-7 1/2". H: 9'-6 1/2" Built 1906–07, Pressed Steel Car Company
14500 to 15499	U9	LOS: 22'-5", W: 8'-11 5/8", H: 9'-6" Built 1913, Western Standard Car and Foundry Company
19000 to 19999	U10	
20001 to 21000	U11	LOS: 22'- 1/2", W: 9'-2 1/8", H: 9' 7" Built 1916, Western Steel Car and Foundry Company
34000 to 34899 and 39000 to 39699		Tapered side cars with ribs LOS: 22'-1", W: 8'-7 1/2", H: 9' Built 1906–07, Pressed Steel Car Company Assigned to work service in 1958 with the prefix W for the car numbers.
41500 to 42299	E8	Slope end cars, LOS: 22', W: 9'-2", H: 9'-6" Built 1913, Standard Steel Car Company
42300 to 42499	E9	Tapered side cars with rib sides LOS: 21'-11", W: 9', H: 9'-7" Built 1913, American Car and Foundry
42500 to 42749	E10	Tapered side cars with rib sides LOS: 21'-11", W: 9', H: 9'-7" Built 1916, American Car and Foundry
42750 to 43249	E11	Smooth side cars with slanted ends LOS: 22'. W: 9'-2", H: 9'-6" Built 1916, Standard Steel Car Company

All of the Class E cars were built for the former Duluth and Iron Range Railway

The 70-ton Ore Car Fleet

Car Numbers	Class	Remarks

21001 to 21026 — U12 — Slanted end car
LOS: 21'-5 1/2", W: 10'-5", H: 10'-2 3/8"
21001 – 21025 built 1925, 21026 in 1929, American Car and Foundry Co.

All of the following cars have rectangular sides unless otherwise noted:

21101 to 21126 — U13 — Rectangular side with three ribs below rectangular section
LOS: 21'-6", W: 10'-6", H: 10'-2"
Built 1925, Pullman Car and Manufacturing Company

22001 to 22125 — U14 — Designed with 3 ribs similar to the U13
LOS: 21'-5 1/2", W: 10'-6", H: 10'-2"
Built 1928, General American Tank Car Company

23001 to 23125 — U15 — Designed with 3 ribs
LOS: 21'-5 1/2", W: 10'-6", H: 10'-2"
Built 1928, Standard Steel Car Company

23171 to 23177 — U16 — The U16 was a rare car with only 7 on the roster
Built in 1923, purchased in 1931, Standard Steel Car Co.

The following group of equipment, Types U17 to U31, was the most common type of ore cars on the DM&IR since the 1950s. The basic dimensions were:

LOS: 21'-6", W: 10'-8 7/8", H: 10'-2"

Car Numbers	Class	Remarks
23975 to 24999	U17	Built 1937-38, Pullman Standard Car Manufacturing Co.
25000 to 25499	U18	Built 1937, General American Tank Car Corporation
25500 to 25999	U19	Built 1942, Pullman Standard Car Manufacturing Co.
26000 to 26499	U20	Built 1942, General American Transportation Co.
26500 to 26499	U21	Built 1942, American Car and Foundry Co.
27000 to 27499	U22	Built 1943, Pressed Steel Car Company
27500 to 27499	U23	Built 1948, Pullman Standard Car Manufacturing Co.
28000 to 28499	U24	Built 1948, American Car and Foundry Co.
28500 to 28999	U25	Built 1948, Pressed Steel Car Co.
29000 to 29499	U26	Built 1948, General American Transportation Co.
29500 to 30499	U27	Built 1949, Pullman Standard Car Manufacturing Co.
30500 to 30999	U28	Built 1949, General American Transportation Co.
31000 to 32499	U29	Built 1952, Pullman Standard Car Manufacturing Co.
32500 to 32999	U30	Built 1953, Pullman Standard Car Manufacturing Co.
33000 to 33499	U31	Built 1957, American Car and Foundry Co.

Equipment Rebuilt with High Side Extensions of 19.5 inches
50031 to 59991 From the U27 to U31 Classes, the cars were rebuilt with
19 1/2-inch extensions. The high side extensions have been replaced with the Mini-quad Group listed below.

Mini-Quads Rebuilt with 9 3/4-inch Extensions
51000 to 53498 From the U29 to U31 Classes

Renumbered Ore Cars from Various Groups
60000 to 61140 New Classification Type: 254

Crude Ore Cars or Thunder Bird Cars
40316 to 40797
49001 to 49008

Ballast Cars Rebuilt from Ore Cars
In 1972, the DM&IR rebuilt two U17 ore cars, 24200 and 24350, with ballast hopper doors. The same year, two cars (former Class U30) with 9 3/4" extensions were also converted to ballast cars, numbers 32675 and 32880. The cars were painted in a yellow scheme with a maroon lettering. Eventually, the company rebuilt 102 cars for ballast service, number series 1400 to 1501, many, but not all, painted yellow with maroon lettering.

The DM&IR has two ore docks in Duluth, Minnesota. This view shows the No. 5 dock, which is now out of service. *Patrick C. Dorin*

The No. 6 ore dock is very active and has had a substantial amount of rebuilding since the 1970s. This view of the No. 6 shows the new conveyor belt system, which can load the wider vessels, as compared to the customary loading chutes, which can be observed to the right of the photo. Also, the pellets are now dumped on the No. 6, either for direct loading into a vessel or for movement to a storage area for a future shipment. A conveyor system handles the pellets to and from the storage area, as well as inbound limestone for fluxing the pellets at the taconite plants. This view shows the Roger Blough loading at the No. 6 ore dock. Several of the conveyor chutes have been lowered for loading the vessel. *Patrick C. Dorin*

This close up view illustrates conveyor chutes No. 22, 24, and 25 lowered for loading the 800-foot ore carrier, the Roger Blough. Note the receiving unit just above the loading chute No. 25. Inbound limestone is unloaded from the vessels with self-unloaders. The limestone is poured into the receiving unit, which then transfers the material by conveyor belt to the storage facility. Later, the limestone is loaded into railroad cars for transportation to the mining facilities for fluxing the pellets. Thus the pellets do not have to be mixed with limestone at the steel making plants since they already contain the appropriate limestone mix. Making steel is like baking a cake, only with a mixture of coke, limestone and iron ore, now mostly pellets. *Patrick C. Dorin*

The DM&IR has three ore docks at Two Harbors, of which two are operational. This view shows the No. 1, which receives the ore loads with switching moves from the ore yard to the dock. *September 2003, Patrick C. Dorin*

The older No. 6 ore dock, the shortest on the Great Lakes with a chute-to-chute length of 888 feet, is now out of service. The approach has been dismantled. If the dock were to be placed back in service in the future, either the rail approach or a conveyor system would have to be built to the dock. *September 2003, Patrick C. Dorin*

The 1,000-foot Presque Isle is shown here at the left side of the No. 2 ore dock. When the larger boats loaded at this side of the dock, they needed to move over to the No. 1 to receive a balance load of ore since the chutes are unable to provide an appropriate cross load on the boat. *Patrick C. Dorin*

The right side of the No. 2 ore dock has been modified with the newer conveyor belt chutes, which permit a full, balanced load into the wider, 1,000-foot carriers. *2003, Patrick C. Dorin*

These two photos illustrate the conveyor belt system that transports the pellets to the No. 2 ore dock. *2003, Patrick C. Dorin*

When the ore trains arrive at the Two Harbors docks, the cars are either unloaded through a car dumper with the pellets moving to a storage area, or they are transferred directly to the ore docks, either No. 1 or 2, for unloading into the pockets. This can take place when the ship can receive the pellets directly from the train load. This view shows the entrance to the car dumper. *2003, Patrick C. Dorin*

As at the Duluth facility, the Two Harbors dock system has a stacker for piling the pellets for storage until a boat arrives for loading. *Patrick C. Dorin*

The pellets are stockpiled according to their chemical content in order to separate the different products, such as fluxed pellets, and also products from the different mining companies. There can be as many as five or six different types of pellets in storage awaiting shipment. *Patrick C. Dorin*

This view shows part of the conveyor belt system for transporting the pellets to the No. 2 ore dock. *Patrick C. Dorin*

The Two Harbors ore yard handles the ore trains for either unloading at the car dumper or for transfer to the ore docks. Switching is minimal since most of the ore and pellet production now comes from only two or three plants, and sometimes natural ores from stockpiles from previously closed mines. *2003, Patrick C. Dorin*

This aerial view of the Duluth docks illustrates the curves and approaches to the No. 5 and 6 docks. The low level dock to the right was a limestone dock that received material for the steel plants that once existed in Duluth. This dock area, as illustrated previously, is now a filled in area for the outbound taconite pellets and the inbound limestone storage for movement to the Mesabi Range for fluxing the pellets. *Basgen Photography, 59407, Dan Mackey Collection*

Here is an interesting photo taken during the 1959 steel strike. Many of the ore vessels were tied up at the Duluth docks. There were four at the No. 5, and nineteen at the No. 6, plus two more at the low level dock. Note the cars on the low level dock to the right. *Basgen Photograph, 59598.1m, Dan Mackey Collection*

To wrap up the section of the DM&IR ore docks, here is a photo from 1910 of the Duluth and Iron Range Two Harbors facilities. This photo illustrates the approaches to the six ore docks. The sixth ore dock is under construction in this photo. The ore cars in the background are a mixture of wooden and steel equipment. Many of the cars are the tapered side 50-ton ore cars and many other designs. The track in the foreground is the outbound track for empty ore trains returning to the Mesabi and Vermilion Iron Ranges. *T100.126.103, Lake Superior Railroad Museum*

This 1925 photo of a Duluth and Iron Range Railway ore train shows a consist of 50-ton ore cars. The first one is a slanted end car (numbers cannot be detected) and the second is a Summers ore car. Diagrams in this chapter provide more information regarding car numbers and other data. *T100.126.88, Lake Superior Railroad Museum*

A train of loaded ore cars from Proctor Yard has just arrived on the No. 5 ore dock in Duluth. DM&IR 2-10-2, No. 605 pulled the train down the hill with the retainers set up for a safe trip down to the ore docks. The photo illustrates a mixed consist of 50- and 70-ton ore cars. Note the first car behind the engine (the engine is moving backward) is a 50-ton rectangular side car. The fourth car is a tapered side car with ribs. The next car is a tapered side 50-ton car with a smooth side. Looking ahead to the ninth car, it is a 70-ton car and one can observe the higher and wider dimensions. A note about the ore train: Once the train has stopped, the engine will uncouple and move to the ore dock to pickup a train of empties. It will then go forward off the dock, move through a crossover and proceed to clear the approach. At the end of the approach, the train will slowly back down through a crossover to pick up the caboose, which was on the rear of the train in this photo. Once the caboose is picked up, the train will proceed back to the Proctor Yard. *T100.126.104, Lake Superior Railroad Museum*

This work train is north of Two Harbors and is equipped with the 50-ton tapered side cars that were converted to work train service. Many of the cars in this work train dumping ballast would be from work car series W8405 to W10554. In 1958, there were 147 cars within this group. The cars were formerly Class U3 cars built between 1905 and 1907. A total of 2,250 cars, numbered 8405 to 10554, were placed in service. Refer to the diagram of this equipment in the introduction. Finally, ore cars were often converted to work equipment on several railroads. *T100.126.75, Lake Superior Railroad Museum*

This roster photo of the Duluth, Missabe and Northern 50-ton ore car, No. 4727, illustrates the lettering for the DM&N in the early days. Note that the air hose is above the coupler, which allowed switchmen to couple the hoses without bending down between the wheels. *Northeast Minnesota Historical Center, University of Minnesota Duluth, S3742 Box 16, Folder 46*

DM&N ore car 12029's portrait was taken in May 1911. The new slope end steel ore cars had already proved to be an effective system for handling iron ore. *Northeast Minnesota Historical Center, UMD, S3742, Box 16, Folder 46*

Car No. 19126 illustrates the development of the 50-ton ore cars to the rectangular side version has shown here. *Northeast Minnesota Historical Center, UMD, S3742, Box 16, Folder 46*

The Duluth, Missabe and Northern began purchasing 70-ton capacity ore cars as early as 1925. DM&N No. 25399 (25000 to 25499) was built by Pressed Steel Car Company in 1937. This was a standard design for many of the DM&N, and later the DM&IR, ore cars. This type of car is still in operation on the DM&IR, now Canadian National, in 2006. *Northern Minnesota Historical Center, UMD, S3742, Box 16, Folder 46*

DM&IR car No 30167, Class U27, (29500 to 30499) was built in 1952 by Pullman Standard Car Manufacturing Company. Note the rivets and how this car matches the Walthers HO gauge ore cars. *Northeast Minnesota Historical Center, UMD, S3742, Box 16, Folder 46*

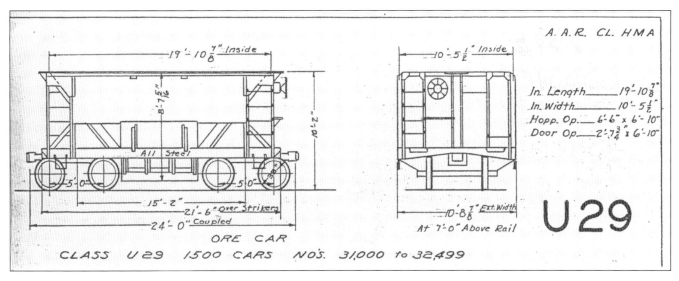

A.A.R. CL. HMA

In. Length _____ 19'-10⅞"
In. Width _____ 10'-5½"
Hopp. Op. _____ 6'-6" x 6'-10"
Door Op. _____ 2'-7¾" x 6'-10"

U29

ORE CAR

CLASS U29 1500 CARS NO'S. 31,000 to 32,499

Diagram for the U29 Class, which illustrates the dimensions for most of the modern DM&IR as illustrated by the 30167 and the DM&N 25399.

These two views by Bob Blomquist illustrate the type of lettering on the DM&IR ore cars from the 1990s and into present time (October 2006).

Some interesting modifications to the ore car fleet took place in the mid-1960s. The cars received 19 1/2-inch extensions to accommodate the need for a greater cubic capacity for the taconite pellets. This photo of the 53409 shows the type of extension, which was eventually replaced by 9 3/4-inch extensions. The rebuilt cars were painted in an attractive maroon color scheme with yellow lettering. At the top of the extension is a line with the words, "Load Limit Line Tac Crude & Pellets Level Full." The ore cars were also used to haul the taconite crude ore from the Thunder Bird mine to the processing plant at Eveleth. The 53409 here is in the consist of a train en route to the Duluth ore docks in 1968.

A number of the ore cars with the extensions were modified with notches, such as the 40103 and the 40299 illustrated here. The cars were known as Thunder Bird ore cars as their assignment was the movement of taconite crude ore to the plant. The 40103 was in the maroon color scheme while the 40299 simply had a partial repaint with the reporting marks and number.

Car No. 52601 shows the 9 3/4-inch extension and also the modified lettering system painted over the insignia. The cars were also coupled together as four car sets. As many modelers know, Walthers also produced the mini-quad sets in the original and subsequent colors and lettering schemes. *May 2001, Robert Blomquist*

The four car sets are known as mini-quads. This is one example of a set of ore cars with notches in the extensions, which meant the cars could also be operated in Thunder Bird service. *Patrick C. Dorin*

This photo illustrates the draw bar connection between the interior three connections for the mini-quad groups. *September 2003, Patrick C. Dorin*

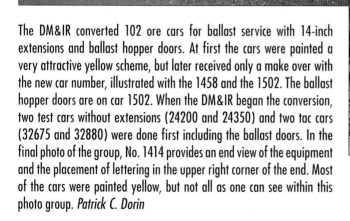

The DM&IR converted 102 ore cars for ballast service with 14-inch extensions and ballast hopper doors. At first the cars were painted a very attractive yellow scheme, but later received only a make over with the new car number, illustrated with the 1458 and the 1502. The ballast hopper doors are on car 1502. When the DM&IR began the conversion, two test cars without extensions (24200 and 24350) and two tac cars (32675 and 32880) were done first including the ballast doors. In the final photo of the group, No. 1414 provides an end view of the equipment and the placement of lettering in the upper right corner of the end. Most of the cars were painted yellow, but not all as one can see within this photo group. *Patrick C. Dorin*

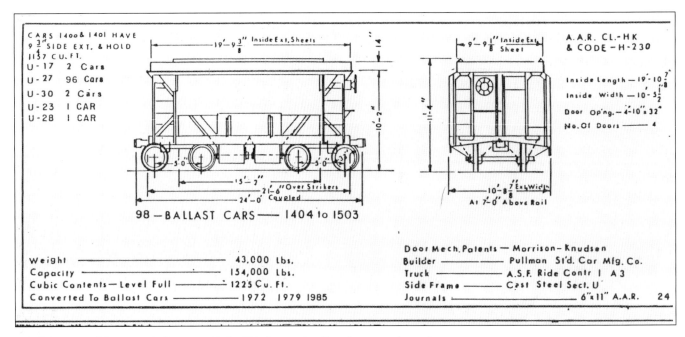

CARS 1400 & 1401 HAVE
9 3/4" SIDE EXT. & HOLD
1137 CU. FT.
U-17   2 Cars
U-27   96 Cars
U-30   2 Cars
U-23   1 CAR
U-28   1 CAR

19'-9 3/8" Inside Ext. Sheets

15'-7"
21'-6" Over Strikers
24'-0" Coupled

5'-0"   5'-0"

10'-2"

14"

98 — BALLAST CARS —— 1404 to 1503

9'-9 1/8" Inside Ext. Sheet

11'-4"

10'-8 7/8" Ext. Width
At 7'-0" Above Rail

A.A.R. CL.-HK
& CODE — H-230

Inside Length — 19'-10 7/8"
Inside Width — 10'-5 1/2"
Door Op'ng. — 4'-10"x32"
No. Of Doors —— 4

Weight ————————————————— 43,000 lbs.
Capacity ———————————————— 154,000 lbs.
Cubic Contents — Level Full ——— 1225 Cu. Ft.
Converted To Ballast Cars ——— 1972 1979 1985

Door Mech. Patents — Morrison-Knudsen
Builder ———————— Pullman St'd. Car Mfg. Co.
Truck ———————— A.S.F. Ride Contr'l A3
Side Frame ———————— Cast Steel Sect. U
Journals ———————————————— 6"x11" A.A.R.   24

DM&IR Diagram of the ore car ballast cars with the 14 inch extension. Note the car number series.

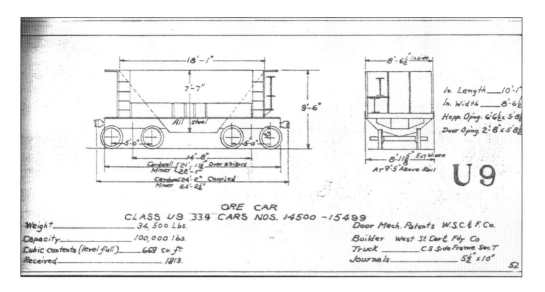

ORE CAR
CLASS U9 334 CARS NOS. 14500 -15499

Weight _____ 34,500 Lbs.	Door Mech. Patents W.S.C.& F. Co.
Capacity _____ 100,000 lbs.	Builder West St Car Fdy Co
Cubic contents (level full) 669 cu. ft.	Truck _____ C.S Side Frame Sec T
Received _____ 1913.	Journals _____ 5½" x 10"

52

In. Length ____ 10'-1"
In. Width ____ 8'-6½
Hopp. Oping. 6'-6½ x 5'-8½
Door Oping. 2'-8 x 5'-8½

U9

We will wrap up this section on the DM&IR ore cars with three diagrams illustrating the Class U9, U11 (50-ton ore cars) and the Class U12. The U12 was an unusual car in that it was a sloped end 70-ton capacity car. The total number of cars was 26, number series 21001 to 21026.

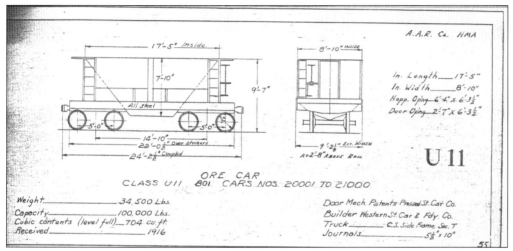

ORE CAR
CLASS U11 801 CARS NOS. 20001 TO 21000

Weight _____ 34,500 Lbs.	Door Mech. Patents Pressed St. Car Co.
Capacity _____ 100,000 Lbs.	Builder Western St. Car & Fdy. Co.
Cubic contents (level full) 704 cu ft.	Truck _____ C.S. Side Frame Sec. T
Received _____ 1916	Journals _____ 5½" x 10"

55

A.A.R. Cl. HMA

In. Length ____ 17'-5"
In. Width ____ 8'-10"
Hopp. Oping. 6'-4" x 6'-3½
Door Oping. 2'-7" x 6'-3½

U 11

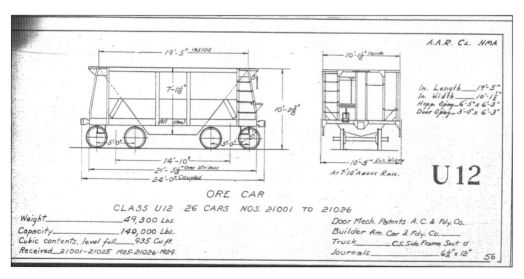

ORE CAR
CLASS U12 26 CARS NOS. 21001 TO 21026

Weight _____ 49,300 Lbs.	Door Mech. Patents A. C. & Fdy. Co.
Capacity _____ 140,000 Lbs.	Builder Am. Car & Fdy. Co.
Cubic contents, level full 935 Cu ft.	Truck _____ C.S. Side Frame Sect. U
Received 21001-21025 1925-21026-1929	Journals _____ 6½" x 12"

56

A.A.R. Cl. HMA

In. Length ____ 19'-5"
In. Width ____ 10'-1½
Hopp. Oping. 6'-5" x 6'-3
Door Oping. 3'-0" x 6'-3

U 12

CHAPTER 2

THE GREAT NORTHERN RAILWAY

The history of ore shipping on the Great Northern Railway began in 1892 with the construction of the first ore dock by the Duluth and Winnipeg Railway in Allouez on the east side of Superior, Wisconsin. The Great Northern purchased the ore dock as such in 1899. Altogether over the next few years through 1911, the GN constructed the largest complex of ore docks on the Great Lakes with the largest total storage capacity. A grand total of four docks were constructed with the longest being 2,244 feet long, and the shortest 1,812 feet long. The ore dock systems are as follows:

The GN Ore Dock System

Ore Dock No. 1

The first ore dock was built by the D&W in 1892. The Great Northern rebuilt the wooden ore dock in 1907 with a 2,244-foot length, 374 pockets, 73 feet high and 63 feet wide. The storage capacity was 112,000 tons.

The GN began a rebuilding process with steel and concrete for the No. 1 during the time period 1925 through 1928. It remained a 2,244-foot long facility, but was now 80 feet, 6 inches high. The 374 pockets each had a capacity of 350 tons for a total ore dock capacity of 130,900 tons.

The No. 1 ore dock received a conveyor belt system in 1967 for handling taconite pellets from the new ground storage area. A car dumper had been constructed for handling the 24-foot modified ore cars with new extensions. The new ground storage area provided an opportunity for ore train operations on a year-round basis. The ore dock could still handle ore car dumping on the dock with the new conveyor system, which could load pellets into the pockets on both sides of the dock. The No. 1 has been inactive for well over a decade as of this writing in 2006, but could be activated for new levels of operation if needed.

Ore Dock No. 2

No. 2 was originally constructed in 1899 as a wooden dock. It was reconstructed with steel and concrete in 1923. The rebuilt dock was 2,100 feet long, 80 feet, 6 inches high above the water, and 56 feet wide with 350 pockets for a total capacity of 122,500 tons at 350 tons per pocket. The No. 2 is currently idle and would require either a conveyor belt system or a rebuilding of the rail ore dock approach to become operational in the future.

Ore Dock No. 3

Great Northern's No. 3 ore dock has an interesting history. It was the only wooden ore dock to remain operational from its construction in 1902 through to the mid-1960s. The ore dock was originally built 960 feet long with 160 pockets. The dock was 77 feet high and 59 feet, 8 inches wide. No. 3 was extended with 166 additional pockets for a grand total of 326 pockets in 1906. The extension increased the length of the ore dock to 1,956 feet with a total storage capacity of 97,800 tons at 300 tons per pocket.

The ore dock received upgrading and rebuilding during the years 1918 through 1921.

The Great Northern No. 3 ore dock became the longest lasting wooden ore dock on the Great Lakes.

Ore Dock No. 4

The final ore dock during the Great Northern history of operations was the No. 4 constructed in steel and concrete in 1911. It was 1,812 feet long, 62 feet, 6 inches wide and 75 feet high. With 302 pockets, the tonnage capacity of the No. 4 was 90,600 tons at 300 tons per pocket.

The Great Northern maintained an ore classification yard for distributing loaded ore cars on the dock according to steel company specifications for ore loads, and the boat scheduling. It was the only "Hump Yard" for ore operations in the Lake Superior Region. At the top of the hump was a scale for weighing each individual car as it went across the hump without stopping. Blocks of cars with different types of ores were sorted out as they went over the hump and designated for certain tracks determined by ore load orders and the boat scheduling. Sometimes the boat scheduling could get fouled up, and one could see vegetation growing on top of the ore loads from time to time. However, that was part of the service provided by the Great Northern for the mines and steel company requirements. The record tonnage for shipping took place in 1953 at 32,330,722 tons.

The four Great Northern docks as a group had the largest storage capacity to be found anywhere in the Lake Superior Region. The total capacity of the four ore docks was 441,800 tons. The second largest capacity was for the two DM&IR docks in Duluth with 268,800 tons while the Northern Pacific ore dock added another 108,500-ton capacity. The grand total was 819,100 tons, which made the three ore dock systems the largest capacity in the world for the Twin Ports of Duluth/Superior.

The Ore Car Fleet

The Great Northern ore car fleet consisted mostly of the 75-ton capacity cars since the 1950s. The cars were painted in a boxcar red type of color with white lettering. One interesting aspect of the GN lettering and number placement was that, at first, the car numbers were painted at the top of the car. Later the numbers were relocated on the bottom of the frame. This made it easier for people to check car numbers when assembling cuts of cars for shoves on the ore dock, and the classification of the different ores at the Allouez ore dock yard and facility.

The rectangular 75-ton ore cars were similar to the DM&IR design discussed earlier in this book. Many of the older 75-ton cars had riveted sides, while the later cars used welded sides. As is known, the GN ore cars were 24 feet long coupled. There were a few minor differences for width, height and length over the strikers.

The following rosters summarize the ore car equipment in service from the early 1950s through the merger in 1970. The information sources include the Great Northern mechanical records and Staffan Ehnbom.

50-ton Ore Cars

Number Series	Remarks
80001 to 80935	Tapered side 50-ton ore cars with 920 cubic feet of capacity.
80937 to 84791	The group included a catwalk around the middle of the car on one side to make it easier for the ore punchers to push the ore out of the car into the pockets on the ore docks.

75-ton Ore Cars

The rectangular side cars and the tapered side cars had a small difference with the dimensions but with the 24-foot length as follows:

Rectangular Side Cars: Length Over Strikers: 20'-2".
Width	10'-6"
Height	10'-2"

Tapered Side Cars: Length Over Strikers: 21'-5 1/2"
Width	10'-3 1/4"
Height	10'-2"

The tapered side car dimensions were the same for the slanted end, tapered side ore cars.

Number Series	Builder	Year	Remarks
85500 to 85800	GN	1930	Rectangular Side
86210 to 86499	Standard Steel	1929	Rectangular Side
86500 to 86999	Bethlehem Steel	1925	Rectangular Side
87000 to 87249	Bethlehem Steel	1924	Tapered Side
87250 to 87999	Bethlehem Steel	1923	Tapered Side
88000 to 88499	AC&F Co.	1920	Tapered Side
88500 to 88999	H&B	1920	Tapered Side with Slanted Ends
89000 to 89748	Pressed Steel	1923	Rectangular Side
90000 to 93499	Several Car Builders		Rectangular Side
	AC&F	1936	
	Bethlehem Steel	1937	
	Pressed Steel Car	1940	
	Bethlehem Steel	1940 and 1942	
	G. A. T. Corp.	1943	
93500 to 94199	AC&F	1953	Rectangular Side
94200 to 94247	GN Railway	1956	Rectangular Side

Rebuilt for Taconite Service

The Taconite ore cars were modified with 20-inch extensions in 1966–67 for the new taconite pellet operations from the two plants served by the Great Northern.

95000 to 95039	Rebuilt from part of the 90000 to 93499 series. This group of cars had riveted rectangular sides.
95500 to 95719	Rebuilt from the car series 93500 to 94199 with welded sides.

This aerial view of the GN (later BN) ore docks shows the No. 1 ore dock in the foreground, which was modified with a conveyor belt system for the transfer of taconite pellets from the ore yard to the dock. The conveyor belt system can be viewed from the lower right section of the photo. It moves along the side and curves upward to the top of the ore dock, which can be observed to the left of the dock office between No. 1 and 2. This photo, although at a distance from the air, is interesting as it includes an ore shove with two units still on the approach for the ore dock. The GN retained flexibility with the No. 1 ore dock for both conveyor and ore car delivery. Note the pilings for the old No. 3 and the new No. 5 dock at the upper right of the photo. No. 5 was built by the Burlington Northern. *Basgen Photography, Dan Mackey Collection*

The conveyor system replaced two of the tracks on the left side of the dock No. 1. A rolling dumper can travel the entire length of belt on the ore dock to divert the pellets from the belt into the pockets. Although somewhat difficult to see in the photo, the pockets to the right are fully loaded with pellets and waiting for the arrival of a boat. At this point in time, 2006, the No. 1 dock is not in operation. *Patrick C. Dorin*

The No. 2 ore dock never received a conveyor system for moving the pellets to the ore dock. Note the car shaker to the left of the photo. The car shaker could be moved over the entire dock. It was used to shake up carloads of iron ore which were wet and sticky, and would not easily slide out of the ore cars into the pockets. *Patrick C. Dorin*

Ore dock No. 3 was the last wooden ore dock on Lake Superior and was dismantled in the late 1960s. Ore dock No. 4 was the shortest of the four ore docks operated by the Great Northern. This view illustrates the four GN ore docks with numbers 1, 2, 3 and 4 from right to left. The GN ore docks were the largest single group of ore docks with the greatest overall capacity on the Great Lakes. *Basgen Photography, Dan Mackey Collection*

The GN ore dock approach went upgrade until reaching the highway U.S. 2 and then contained a steel trestle for part of the distance to the four approaches for the four ore docks. An SD unit is shoving a cut of ore cars to the docks in this photo.

The Great Northern Railway operated the larger 75-ton ore cars and replaced all of the former 50-ton cars by the 1940s. It could be said that the Great Northern had the most modern fleet in terms of tonnage capacity of all of the Lake Superior Region ore lines. Car No. 91346 is an example of the riveted rectangular side cars. These were similar in many respects to the DM&IR ore cars with the same type of rivet arrangements. The Walthers HO gauge model ore car fits this particular Great Northern design. *Patrick C. Dorin*

This diagram shows the dimensions for the 90000 to 93499 series ore cars, which included the 91346. *GN Diagram, Patrick C.*

The Great Northern also operated a fleet of tapered side ore cars. In fact, there were at least three types, one of which had slanted ends. The GN tapered side cars did not have the same type of indented lip at the top of the car side, which made the cars different from other tapered side equipment operated on the Lake Superior and Ishpeming Railroad and the Chicago and North Western. The GN's vertical end equipment was of two basic types. GN 87570 (87250 to 87999) illustrates the cars with rectangular panels at the upper corners of the equipment. *Bob Blomquist*

The 87250 series was built in 1923, and is one of the earliest of the 75-ton capacity cars. *GN Diagram*

GN 87195 (87000 to 87249), had triangular panels at the upper corners of the cars, and was built in 1924. These two sets of 75-ton capacity cars had different side ribs as well. Note the differences and types of ribs on the 87570 and the 87195. *Patrick C. Dorin*

Even with some of the differences, note that the dimensions are the same for both types of these 75-ton ore cars. *GN Diagram*

Built by Bethlehem Steel Co.·1924

19'-10" STEEL ORE CAR Nos. 87000 to 87249
(All Steel)

MRA 500487.
AFE 26422, 6517 7-78, 69523.

HMA

Weight	40300 Lbs.	Side Bearings	Top Hung	Barber Roller	Length (Inside) at top	19'-10"	Brake Step	Steel
Capacity (Nom.)	150000 "	Truck Bolster	Cast Steel	Width (Inside)	9'-9 5/8"	Poking Platform	Steel
Draft Gear _ G-20	Cardwell	Kind Of Truck	Andrews			
Coupler _ AAR Type D	6 1/8"	Journal Size	6"x11"	Cubic Capacity-Level Full	892 Cu. Ft.	
Centering Device	None	Wheels _ Rolled Steel	33"	-12" Heap	1080 "	
Yokes	Cast Steel	Snubbers	Yes		
Release _ Type B	Imperial	Brake Beam _ No.2 Plus			
Air Brake _ A B	10"x12"	Support _ 3rd Pt.	Creco	Door Rigging	National	
Handbrake _ Universal	Power	Slack Adjuster	None		

GN ore car No. 88841 illustrates the slanted end 75-ton ore cars, which were built in 1920. The car name and numbers were painted out as the equipment was being scrapped. These interesting ore cars had three channel ribs center, and hat ribs at the end.

The slanted end 75-ton capacity ore cars were numbered 88500 to 88999. *GN Diagram*

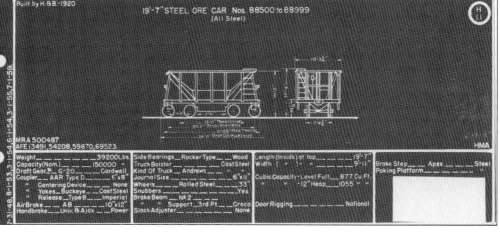

Built by H. B.B.-1920

19'-7" STEEL ORE CAR Nos. 88500 to 88999
(All Steel)

MRA 500487.
AFE 13491, 54208, 59870, 69523.

HMA

Weight	39200 Lbs.	Side Bearings _ Rocker Type	Wood	Length (Inside) at top	19'-7"	Brake Step _ Apex	Steel
Capacity (Nom.)	150000 "	Truck Bolster	Cast Steel	Width (")	9'-11"	Poking Platform	
Draft Gear _ G-20	Cardwell	Kind Of Truck _ Andrews				
Coupler _ AAR Type D	6"x8"	Journal Size	6"x11"	Cubic Capacity-Level Full	877 Cu. Ft.	
Centering Device	None	Wheels _ Rolled Steel	33"	-12" Heap	1055 "	
Yokes _ Buckeye	Cast Steel	Snubbers	Yes		
Release _ Type B	Imperial	Brake Beam _ No 2			
Air Brake _ A B	10"x12"	Support _ 3rd Pt.	Creco	Door Rigging	National	
Handbrake _ Univ. & Ajax	Power	Slack Adjuster	None		

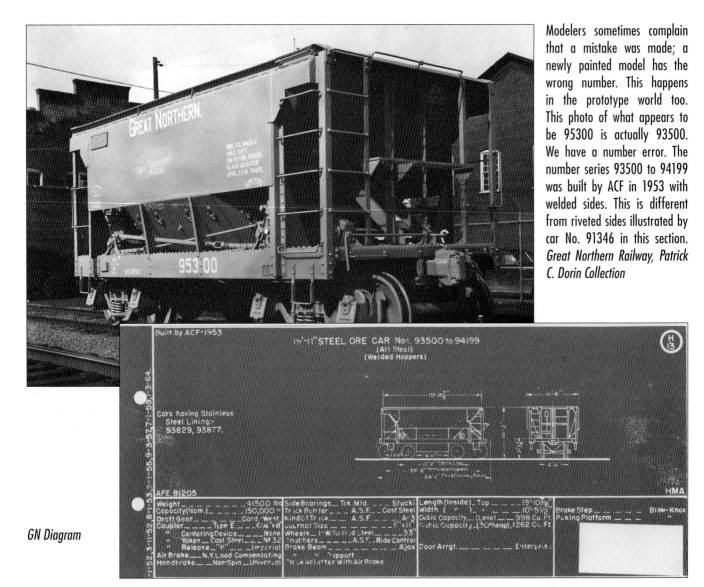

Modelers sometimes complain that a mistake was made; a newly painted model has the wrong number. This happens in the prototype world too. This photo of what appears to be 95300 is actually 93500. We have a number error. The number series 93500 to 94199 was built by ACF in 1953 with welded sides. This is different from riveted sides illustrated by car No. 91346 in this section. *Great Northern Railway, Patrick C. Dorin Collection*

GN Diagram

GN No. 92673 (another example of the 90000 series) was built in 1942 and lasted in active service into the 1970s. When many of the GN ore cars were built, the car numbers were placed at the top of the car. Later, they were repainted at the bottom of the frame. Note the riveted sides. *Robert Blomquist*

GN No. 95617 (95500 to 95719) was part of the taconite car fleet, most of which were built with welded sides and did not have the customary rivets. The cars were painted in a color similar to boxcar red with the white lettering and the yellow ends for appropriate spotting at the car dumpers. The GN cars for Taconite service, number series 95000 to 95039, were rebuilt from the 90000 to 93499 with riveted sides. *Robert Blomquist*

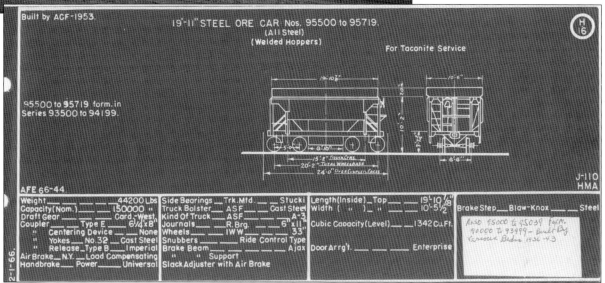

The cars were rebuilt with 20-inch extensions, which lasted throughout the BN era and were not rebuilt with 9 3/4-inch extensions as happened on the DM&IR. *GN Diagram*

The rebuilt ore cars had a full yellow paint scheme on the extension on one side, while it was only at the end as illustrated on car 95617. Note how the yellow ends were coupled together as this train moves through a taconite pellet loading facility at Nashwauk, Minnesota, on Mother's Day, 1967. The yellow painted sections were lined up at the appropriate point within the Allouez car dumpers for unloading the cars. *Patrick C. Dorin*

CHAPTER 3

THE NORTHERN PACIFIC RAILWAY

The Northern Pacific began ore hauling traffic operations in 1913 when they began construction on their one and only ore dock in Superior, Wisconsin. The railroad served the Cuyuna Range about 100 miles west of the Twin Ports of Duluth/Superior.

The ore was transported from the Ironton, Minnesota, area over the company's main line operation to Superior.

The NP Ore Dock

The Northern Pacific constructed their only steel and concrete ore dock in 1913. The company never did build or operate a wooden ore dock as virtually all of the other ore haulers did in Minnesota and Michigan. What is interesting about the NP ore dock is that it was built in three stages as follows:

1913 The first section was 612 feet long and 80 feet high with 102 pockets for a 35,700-ton storage capacity.

1917 The next phase was an extension of the ore dock by 600 feet with 100 additional pockets providing an additional 35,000 tons in capacity.

1926 The final phase was another extension of 648 feet with 108 pockets and 37,800 more tons in storage capacity.

The total length of the ore dock was 1,860 feet long with a total storage capacity of 108,500 tons in a grand total of 310 pockets.

As of 1929, the NP and the Soo Line Railroad joined together for a pool service operation to the Cuyuna Range. Thus the mixture of ore cars to be observed on the ore dock came from both the Soo Line and the NP. For the most part, NP power provided the switching service for the ore dock operations. However, as part of the pooling agreement, Soo Line crews were often operating the NP power.

The NP ore dock continued in operation until 1969. As of 1970, and the BN merger, the NP dock was closed and all Cuyuna Range iron ores were shifted over to the former Great Northern ore docks, now part of the Burlington Northern System, the topic of Chapter 4.

The NP Steel Ore Car Fleet

The NP ore car fleet consisted of both 50- and 70-ton ore cars. The cars were painted black with white lettering and numbers on the chassis. The fleet consisted entirely of rectangular side cars in both the 50- and 70-ton capacity groups. The fleet from the 1950s through the 1970 merger is as follows:

This photo illustrates the west side of the NP ore dock in Superior. The facility located at the end of the wooden approach was the office for handling the car dumping, loading boats, and dock maintenance. *Gary Wildung*

The Northern Pacific ore dock handled the traffic from the Cuyunna Range with the Soo Line and the NP ore pooling agreement. The trains were a mixture of Soo Line and NP ore cars. In this photo, the NP 2-8-2 is shoving a mixture of Soo and NP ore cars onto the dock. The NP and the Soo also interchanged ore with the DM&IR and the Great Northern, so it was not uncommon to have ore cars from all four railroads in the NP ore yard and on the ore dock. This photo illustrates the final segment of the wooden trestle and the steel bridge approach to the dock. *Gary Wildung*

The Ore Car Roster 1950 to 1970
50-ton Cars

Number Series	Remarks
79100 to 79998	By the mid-1960s, there was but one 50-ton ore car remaining on the roster, the 79306. In 1956, the NP still operated 298 50-ton cars, which were mixed with the Soo Line cars in the ore pool operations.
	The length over the strikers for the 50-ton cars was 22'-1". The extreme width was 8'-11" while the height was 11'-1".

70-ton Cars

Number Series	Remarks
77800 to 77999	Built by the NP in 1957 in Brainerd, Minnesota, with square corners and welded sides. Length over strikers was 21'-5 1/2" and width was 10'-6 7/8" with a 10'-5 5/6" height.
78000 to 78199	Similar to GN ore cars with welded sides, but not identical. LOS: 21' 7 1/2", W: 10' 4 3/4" H: 10'-2" Built 1924, Pullman Standard Car Company
78300 to 78699	Built at the NP Shops in Brainerd, Minnesota in 1950.
78700 to 78899	Built by the NP in 1954 with square corners as the 77800 to 77999 series, which was built later.

These two groups were 21'-6" long over the strikers and 10'-3" high. The 78300 series was 10'-10" wide while the 78700 group was 10'-8" wide. The total number of ore cars in 1956 included 298 fifty-ton cars and 797 seventy-ton cars for a total of 1,095, compared with 954 seventy-ton cars only in 1968.

This aerial shows the NP ore dock to the north of the Great Northern ore docks in Superior. *Basgen Photography, No. 53073, Dan Mackey Collection*

This NP ore shove consists of DM&IR ore cars. The engine is working hard to maintain the shove, but at the same time keeping the consist under control for appropriate placement on the ore dock. Although this writer is not aware of accidents of cars being pushed over the end of the NP dock, there are stories of it happening on other railroads. *Wayne Olson, Gary Wildung Collection*

NP ore car 78899 was part of the last group of ore cars acquired by the railroad. Note the welded sides and the square corners. Many of these cars were later rebuilt by the BN with extensions for taconite service. *Robert Blomquist*

This photo illustrates two of the three basic types of 75-ton ore cars operated on the NP. The first car, 78490, has welded sides, while the second car illustrates the riveted sides that were common on the GN and the DM&IR. The third car is a Great Northern ore car. The cars were in coal delivery service to a coal and oil fuel yard in North Branch, Minnesota, in the early 1970s. *Patrick C. Dorin*

NP 78536 is a welded side car with a different type of support ribs below the rectangular side. The car is shown here in coal service at Duluth, Minnesota. *Gary Wildung*

Among the earliest 70-ton cars ordered by the NP were the 78000 – 78199 series in 1924. The cars were built by Pressed Steel Car Company. *NP Diagram*

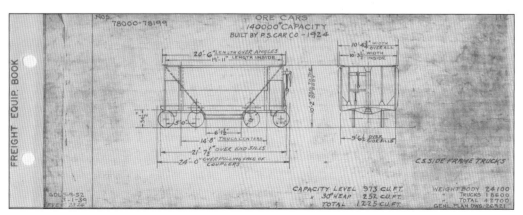

BURLINGTON NORTHERN & SANTA FE RAILROAD

The Burlington Northern was an outcome of one of James J. Hill's dreams of a century ago to fuse together the Northern Pacific, the Great Northern and the Burlington into one empire. The merger took place in 1970, which brought a major change in the GN and NP ore operations. As mentioned in Chapter 4, the NP dock was shut down and all ore shipping went to the BN's GN facilities. The former Great Northern had already converted the No. 1 ore dock with a conveyor belt system for feeding the expanding traffic of taconite pellets. As the natural iron ore traffic dwindled over the 1970s, the BN set in motion a plan for a new ore dock with a conveyor feeding system for the dock as well as an expanded storage area. The ore dock system had been substantially modified. Eventually, only the new No. 5 dock was in operation but the No. 1 can be reactivated if needed with its conveyor systems.

The BNSF Ore Dock System

Dock No. 1
No. 1 has been inactive for several years, but is still connected with a conveyor belt system to the storage and dumper systems. For specifications refer to Chapter 2, the Great Northern Railway dock systems.

Docks No. 2 and 4
Ore docks 2 and 4 are still in existence but have been disconnected from the railroad ore yard. The two docks never acquired a conveyor belt system. If the two docks were to be placed back in operation, either a conveyor belt system would have to be constructed, or the rail ore dock approaches reinstalled.

Dock No. 5
The No. 5 ore dock was built in 1977, ten years after the Great Northern had modified dock No. 1 for the conveyor belt systems. The new dock is a silo type of facility with 36 silos, 18 on each side, 130 feet high. The dock is 900 feet long silo-to-silo length. The total pellet storage capacity of No. 5 is 72,000 tons.
There are 18 retractable conveyor loading chutes, one for each pair of silos, for loading the ore vessels. They are mounted 45 feet above the lake and can be extended 65 feet out over the vessel to load pellets.
Dock No. 5 is fed from two storage areas located in the former Great Northern Allouez ore yard. The total storage area capacity for pellets is 5.5 million tons. There

are two dumping stations. Trains of 180 100-ton ore cars can be unloaded in about 5 hours at the new dumper, and about 8 hours at the older dumper originally built by the Great Northern before the BN merger. The BNSF ore dock system is capable of handling over 15 million tons of pellets annually depending upon the weather and boat scheduling.

The Ore Car Fleet
The BN ore car fleet was an outgrowth of the Great Northern and Northern Pacific fleet of ore cars in 1970. The GN had already converted a fleet of cars with extensions for the new taconite pellet service. As the BN merger progressed, the company converted additional GN and NP cars with extensions. The color schemes of boxcar red with yellow trim followed the Great Northern design for spotting and unloading the 24-foot cars at the dumping station. (See photos)

The Burlington Northern and Santa Fe, as we move into the 21st Century, has only one ore dock in operation. The No. 5 was built by the Burlington Northern and is a silo type of dock with a conveyor belt feeder system. This shows the rear side of the dock and how the conveyor belt system moves to the rear for boat clearance as they arrive and depart. *Thomas A. Dorin*

Table 1

The BN 24-foot Ore Car Fleet for Taconite Service
Fully Repainted with the BN Insignia
75-ton Capacity Cars

Car Numbers	Former GN/NP Number Series	Remarks
95006 to 95037	GN 95006 to 95037	Riveted side cars very close to the Walthers HO gauge ore cars.
95500 to 95839	GN 95500 to 95839	Welded side cars
95840 to 96043	NP 77800 to 77999	Last NP ore cars built with square corners.
96044 to 96085	GN 93500 to 94199	

Table 2

Burlington Northern 100-ton Capacity Ore Cars

Car Numbers	Year Built	Qty	Builder and Remarks
99000 to 99399	1976	200	Bethlehem Steel
		200	Pacific Car and Foundry
99400 to 99699	1980	300	Bethlehem Johnstown
99700 to 99799	1981	100	Bethlehem Johnstown Built in Groups of 4 called "Quads" for a total of 25 sets
99800 to 99949	1988	150	Bethlehem Johnstown
98000 to 98099	1992	100	Johnstown America
98100 to 98189	1995	90	Johnstown America

These BN ore cars are now being relettered with the BNSF reporting marks.

Burlington Northern & Santa Fe 100-ton Ore Cars

Number Series	Year Built	Qty	Builder and Remarks
601090 to 601179	1996	90	Johnstown America With TSM Electric Brake Systems
601180 to 601399	1998	220	Johnstown America With New York Electric Brake Systems
600000 to 600374	1998	230	BN cars rebuilt from groups built in 1976–1980. The rebuilt cars originally had covers, which were eventually removed and placed back in service for the Mesabi Range Taconite Operations.

The BN/BNSF ore cars are 35 feet long over the couplers, 11 feet longer than the 24-foot ore cars. See the following photos for the BN/BNSF ore car fleet as we move into the 21st Century.

This view shows the BNSF No. 5 ore dock from the dock side on a pleasant autumn day. The 1,000-footer, the Mesabi Miner, is taking on a load of taconite pellets. *Basgen Photography, Dan Mackey Collection*

When the train service to the new taconite mines and plants began in the mid-1960s on the Mesabi Range, the trains gained a new name, "The Tac Trains." This name has prevailed over the past forty years plus. A tac train is shown here at the Allouez facility, where there are two loops serving two car dumping facilities. *Patrick C. Dorin*

The GN had constructed one car dumper at the Allouez ore yard, and later the Burlington Northern built the second. This photo by Robert Blomquist illustrates the entry to one of the car dumpers. The pellets then travel by a conveyor belt system to either a stockpile, or directly to the No. 5 ore dock.

BN tac car No. 99099 was built in 1976 and was part of the 99000 to 99399 series. These were the first group of 100-ton capacity ore cars, which were 35 feet long, 11 feet, 7 inches high, and 10 feet, 8 inches wide. *Robert Blomquist*

Tac car 98152 (Series 98000 to 98189) was built in 1995. This larger ore car eventually completely replaced the original 24-foot ore cars. *Robert Blomquist*

BN No. 99757C was part of a group of tac cars that were semi-coupled together as quads. The cars had yellow striping at the one end of the car. The cars each had a different number but with the additional lettering in the consist as A, C, C, B. The A and B cars had regular couplers at the ends, while the interior set of coupling was done with drawbars. The 25 four car sets were numbered 99700 to 99799. *Robert Blomquist*

Many of the BN cars were given extensions at the ends of the equipment to prevent pellets from rolling out of the cars and over the ends. BN 99365 illustrates this type of extension. *Patrick C. Dorin*

Before looking over the repainting and lettering of the tac cars for the Burlington Northern and Santa Fe, let's take a quick look back at the ex-GN and NP ore cars painted and lettered for the BN. BN 78327 was one of only four ore cars in the BN lettering that did not have extensions. *Robert Blomquist*

BN 95755 illustrates the former ore cars rebuilt with extensions. These were much higher than the DM&IR's extensions, 18 inches as compared to 9 3/4 inches respectively. *Robert Blomquist*

The GN, later BN, rebuilt ore cars received yellow ends, which were coupled next to each other for the purpose of spotting two cars at a time in the dumping facilities. This group of cars has been switched out and so one does not observe the correct placement of the yellow ends next to each other. The cars were in storage at the 21st Street Yard in Superior. *Robert Blomquist*

BN 24-foot taconite ore car 96004 (95840 to 96043) was rebuilt from a group of Northern Pacific cars with square corners, number series 77800 to 77999. The cars appear to have just arrived at Allouez to resume their ore service after rebuilding. The date is May 9, 1981. *Robert Blomquist*

With the Burlington Northern and Santa Fe merger, the ore cars have been receiving new reporting marks, BNSF, and new numbers. Car 600032 also illustrates the extension. *Patrick C. Dorin*

This photo of BNSF 600319 illustrates both ends of this type of ore car including the placement of the lettering and numbers. As we move into the latter part of the first decade of the 21st Century, the BNSF has dropped their insignia with the name of the railroad, and has replaced it with a simple BNSF. *Patrick C. Dorin*

Equipment ordered by the BNSF was numbered in the 600000 to 600374 and 601090 to 601399 series. Tac car 601091 was part of the first group built in 1996. The car is in service at Superior in the November 1998 portrait. *Robert Blomquist*

BNSF 601152 only carried the reporting marks and did not include an insignia as illustrated on the previous cars. *Robert Blomquist*

Tac car No. 601146 with the full insignia. Built in 1996 by Johnstown America. *Robert Blomquist*

One rather interesting event was the placement of covers on a group of tac cars for a specialized ore service that was sensitive to rain and other weather elements. The potential traffic never happened, and consequently the equipment had their covers removed and the cars returned to taconite service. *October 1998, Robert Blomquist*

CHAPTER 5

THE SOO LINE RAILROAD

The Soo Line Railroad operated a grand total of four ore shipping ports in the Lake Superior region, but not at the same time. The ports included Gladstone and Marquette in Michigan and Ashland and Superior in Wisconsin. Parts of the operations were acquired because of leasing the Wisconsin Central and the merger with the Duluth, South Shore and Atlantic Railroad. (See Chapter 6)

The Soo Line ore operation began with the Milwaukee Road ore hauling from the Menominee Range in northern Michigan. The railroad built a single, low-level pocket type of ore dock at Gladstone, Michigan. This was a relatively short-lived operation from 1887 through 1901 when the Milwaukee Road built their first ore dock in Escanaba. (See Chapter 7 for the Milwaukee Road.)

The Wisconsin Central was leased by the Soo Line Railroad in 1909, and at the same time the Soo Line acquired a timber ore dock in Ashland, Wisconsin, which was later replaced by a new concrete facility. The Soo Line ore operations continued in Ashland through 1965.

Ore traffic from the Cuyuna Range in central Minnesota flowed over the Soo Line Railroad to Superior, Wisconsin, where the railroad constructed the longest wooden ore dock to be operated on the Great Lakes. Ore operations began on the Cuyuna Range in 1911.

The Soo Line Ore Dock Systems

Superior

The Soo Line constructed one timber ore dock in Superior, Wisconsin, which was 2,412 feet long. Based on the 12-foot centers for the pockets, the ore dock contained 101 pockets on each side for a grand total of 202. The ore dock remained in operation until 1929 when the Soo and the Northern Pacific created an ore pooling agreement, with Soo Line traffic operating over the newer NP dock.

The Soo Line dock and ore yard were constructed to the west of the Great Northern Railway's freight yard complex in Billings Park on the west side of Superior.

Ashland

The Wisconsin Central built the first timber ore dock on the east side of Ashland.

The WC dock was constructed in 1888 and was 1,800 feet long. The ore dock burned in 1900, and for a while the WC sent their ore traffic through the C&NW docks in Ashland.

It is believed that the WC dock was rebuilt as their No. 1.

The Soo Line leased the WC in 1909. The timber ore dock No. 1 was replaced by the new concrete No. 2 ore dock in 1917. The first segment of the dock was 900 feet long with 150 pockets. An additional 900 feet was constructed in 1924 bringing the total number of pockets to 300 with a 105,000-ton storage capacity.

The ore dock and approach were still standing in Ashland as this was being written in early 2006. However, during the fall of 2006, the approach was dismantled. A new mine may open east of Mellen, Wisconsin, and there are ore deposits south and southwest of Ashland, so who knows what the future will bring in terms of ore traffic for northern Wisconsin.

Gladstone

The Gladstone ore dock was built in 1887. The dock was 768 feet long with pockets on one side only. The ore dock was operated for twelve years until the start of the 20th century when the Milwaukee Road decided to build its own ore handling facility in Escanaba, Gladstone's next-door neighbor. This came about because an ore boat struck the dock in the middle, breaking it in two. The ore dock fell and was never repaired.

Marquette

The DSS&A merged with the Soo Line in 1961, and this brought the Soo Line officially to Marquette, Michigan. The DSS&A operated a 900-foot ore dock in Marquette, which was built in 1931. It was the second last pocket ore dock built on Lake Superior. (See Chapter 6)

The Soo Line Ore Car Fleet

The Soo Line ore car fleet was a mixture of 50 and 70/75-ton ore cars until the very end of the ore operations in the early 1980s. It should be mentioned that the last few months of the operations were handled with a fleet of leased ore cars from the DM&IR.

The Soo purchased and built the last group of ore cars during the 1950s. Most of the fleet was the 50-ton cars, of which there were at least three different types. The following roster is an overview of the ore car fleet during the 1950s. The 50-ton capacity cars were also 24 feet, 6 inches long, coupled length.

50-ton Ore Cars

Number Series	Remarks
25701 to 26699	Slanted end cars LOS: 22', W: 10' 4", H: 9' 8"
80000 to 80199	LOS: 22'-1/2", W: 9'-2", H: 9'-5 1/4" Built 1910, Standard Steel Car Company Summers Ore Car
80200 to 80499	Rectangular side ore cars with side braces LOS: 22', W: 9'-9", H: 10'
80500 to 80507	Slanted end cars
80508 to 80807	Slanted end cars LOS: 22', W: 9'-8 5/8", H: 9' 8" Built 1913, American Car and Foundry

80669 to 81599   Slanted end cars
LOS: 21'-5", W: 10'-3 1/8", H: 9'-8"
Built 1920, Haskell and Barker Car Co. Michigan City, Indiana.
80 cars within this group were modified with 7-inch extensions increasing the cubic feet level full from 672 to791.

Examples of Car Numbers with the 7-inch extensions:
80717, 80825, 81139, 81526, 81452
80749, 80975, 81206, 81430, 81101

For a complete list of this equipment with extensions, one may wish to check an Official Railway Equipment Register published from 1956 to 1960.

75-ton Ore Cars

81600 to 81724	Tapered side car built by Pullman in 1925
81725 to 81849	Tapered side car built by AC&F in 1925 LOS: 21'-6 1/2", W: 10'-6", H: 10'-2 1/4" Coupled length: 24'- 7 1/8"

70-ton Ore Cars

81850 to 82049	Rectangular side car with welded sides Built by Soo Line in 1950. LOS: 21'-5 3/8", W: 10'-6", H: 10'-2" Coupled length: 24 feet

The Soo Line ore dock was built in two 900-foot stages. This Soo Line photo shows the 900-foot dock with the construction for the additional 900 feet starting during the spring of 1924. *Soo Line Railroad Photo*

The Soo Line ore dock has not seen any ore traffic since the mid-1960s. This view shows the right side of the ore dock, plus the foundations for the former timber ore dock to the right. *2003, Patrick C. Dorin*

The ore dock approach was built of wood with a concrete section to the ore dock itself. *2003, Patrick C. Dorin*

This view shows the left side of the ore dock. Notice the trees growing out of the foundation. A dock to the left in the photo, although not visible, was once operated for pulpwood traffic arriving in Ashland by barge. *2003, Patrick C. Dorin*

The Soo Line owned and operated two basic types of 70/75-ton capacity ore cars. One group was the tapered side cars, such as the 81844 (81725 to 81849) built by American Car and Foundry in 1925. Note the channel ribs at the ends of the tapered side, which differed from the cars built by Pullman the same year, which had hat ribs at each end with the three channel ribs in the middle. *Patrick C. Dorin*

The Soo Line ore diagram for the tapered side ore cars illustrates the Pullman-built equipment with the placement of the two different types of ribs. The Pullman-built group number series was 81600 to 81724. *Soo Line diagram*

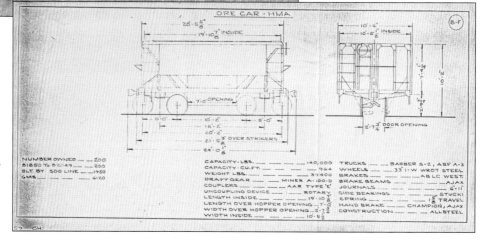

The rectangular side ore cars, such as the 81955, were built by the Soo Line in 1950. The 70- and 75-ton ore cars were operated for the Cuyunna Range ores, which were shipped through the port of Superior over the Northern Pacific ore dock. *Patrick C. Dorin*

Rectangular side ore cars 81850 to 82049. *Soo Line diagram*

The Soo Line also operated 50-ton ore cars into the 1960s, and even into the 1970s. One example was the rectangular side ore car No. 80344. This type of car saw service on all three iron ranges served by the Soo Line, the Cuyunna, the Gogebic and the Marquette. Note the WC in the upper left corner of the ore cars for Wisconsin Central. *Owen Leander, William Raia Collection*

The slanted end 50-ton ore cars were quite interesting. At one time, the cars had a full Soo Line lettering on the side of the cars, but this was later replaced by a nameplate as illustrated with the 80658. This equipment too operated on all of the iron ranges served by the Soo Line. The portraits of the 80344 and the 80658 were taken at North Fon du Lac, Wisconsin, in 1965. *Owen Leander, William Raia Collection*

Slanted end 50-ton ore car, number series 80598 to 80807. *Soo Line diagram*

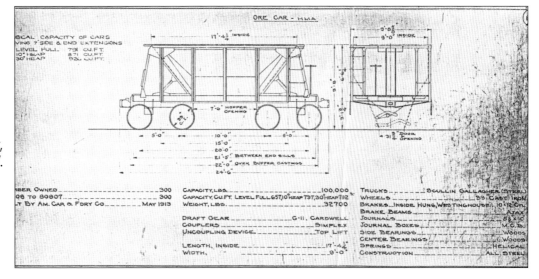

As a final note on Soo Line ore cars, the company also owned and operated Summers ore cars, which were identical to the Duluth, South Shore and Atlantic Railroad ore cars illustrated in Chapter 6, including a diagram. This type of car was operated by the Soo Line, DSS&A and the Duluth, Missabe and Northern with some stretching into eventual Duluth, Missabe and Iron Railway.

CHAPTER 6

THE DULUTH, SOUTH SHORE & ATLANTIC RAILROAD

The DSS&A was an important ore hauler for a variety of mines on the Marquette Range with the ore being shipped through the Marquette ore dock. The railroad handled ore from mines from as far west as near Champion, Michigan, which also happened to be an interchange point with the Milwaukee Road for freight traffic and through passenger trains between Calumet, Michigan, and Chicago. An example of the latter was the Copper Country Limited. The DSS&A was a very colorful railroad, both in the days of steam and the incredible yellow color schemes of the diesel power. The company was ultimately merged into the Soo Line Railroad, and the ore business history came to an end by the 1970s.

The Ore Dock Systems

The ore dock history on the DSS&A goes back as far as 1872. At that time, the Marquette, Houghton and Ontonagon Railroad built an ore dock with a 6,000-ton capacity at L'Anse for Marquette Range iron ores. But that was only the start of the ore dock systems constructed by predecessors of the DSS&A.

The Detroit, Mackinac and Marquette Railroad built an ore dock at St. Ignace in 1882. The very next ore dock showed up at Marquette a year later with a dock constructed by the Marquette and Western. But that was not the first ore dock to be built in Marquette. All three of these railroads were eventually folded into the DSS&A.

One of the first ore docks built at the DSS&A site in Marquette took place in 1855. The Jackson Iron Company built a trestle into the Marquette Harbor. It was the first dock over which iron ore was loaded into boats and the first served by the old scrap iron railroad which operated very small cars of ore from the Jackson Mine in Negaunee. The motive power was a group of mules.

The next dock was constructed by the Lake Superior Iron Company. It was a combination ore and merchandise and as reported in the October 27, 1956, issue of the Skillings Mining Review, it was the first dock built on Lake Superior with pockets and chutes. The dock was destroyed by fire in 1868 and never rebuilt.

One of the next ore docks to be built in Marquette was constructed in 1864 according to the October 27, 1956, issue of Skillings Mining Review. This dock was constructed by the Bay de Noquet and Marquette Railroad. It was a combined ore and merchandise dock.

This dock was 35 feet high with a capacity of nearly 4,000 tons. This dock was destroyed by the 1868 fire but rebuilt by the same railroad in 1869.

The Marquette and Western Railroad built an ore dock in 1883.

The DSS&A constructed an ore dock in 1890, but it was dismantled in 1910 when the Marquette Dock Company constructed a coal dock

The DSS&A constructed a full wooden ore dock with pockets and chutes, and it would fit the modern design of ore loading docks. It was known as Dock No. 5.

The DSS&A built one of the latest ore docks, the No. 6, in 1931. The company constructed a 900-foot dock with 150 pockets, 75 pockets on each side. The dock was built of steel and concrete and had a 56,250-ton capacity. The dock was the highest of all the ore docks ever constructed with the top deck being 85 feet, 7 inches above the water. The dock also featured the greatest height above the water line for the hinge pin of the loading spouts, 43 feet, 3 inches, which made it a fast loading ore dock. In fact, many vessels were loaded within 60 minutes right throughout the 1950s and '60s.

The No. 6 ore dock played a major role for ore shipments for nearly four decades. In addition, the DSS&A handled a substantial amount of ore that needed to be mixed with ores handled by the Lake Superior and Ishpeming Railroad. Consequently, one could see sets of DSS&A and LS&I ore cars on the dock just about at any time. The LS&I delivered their ore traffic to the South Shore yard along the lake front next to the downtown area.

The DSS&A was merged with the Soo Line in 1961, with the company losing its name that had been around for decades. The DSS&A ore dock stood in place for many years without any ore shipments. The approach to the dock was finally taken down in 2001. Now the dock stands as a lonely environment in Marquette.

The DSS&A Ore Car Fleet

The South Shore modern ore cars consisted of a wide variety of 50-ton capacity cars. The company never did own any of the 70- or 75-ton capacity cars that could be found on the C&NW and the LS&I as well as the Soo Line Railroad.

The roster of cars included:

Number Series	Type	Builder	Date
9000 to 9399	Tapered side Full sides	American Car & Foundry	1913

Remarks: LOS: 22'-3 3/4", W: 9'- 1 1/2" H: 10' 2", Coupled Length: 25'
These cars were similar to Chicago and North Western 50-ton capacity ore cars.

Number Series	Type	Builder	Date
9400 to 9489 9509 to 9524 DSS&A Class U4 Formerly Duluth, Missabe & Northern Railway ore cars	Tapered side	Pressed Steel	1906–07

Number Series	Type	Builder	Date
9525 to 9622 9624 to 9667 9669 to 9674 DSS&A Class U-7	Summers ore car	Standard Steel Car	1910

Refer to Soo Line Summers ore car for the specifications. The cars were purchased from the Duluth, Missabe and Northern Railway in 1926.

The ore car fleet continued in service until the very end of the DSS&A Soo Line ore operations on the Marquette Range.

The 900-foot ore dock stretched out into the lake at Marquette, and was a landmark of the city for many years. The DSS&A dock was the second last ore pocket ore dock to be constructed on Lake Superior, the last being the Canadian National at Port Arthur, now known as Thunder Bay. The approach extended through the downtown section of Marquette, and was a great place to watch shoves on to the dock and shopping at the same time. *Patrick C. Dorin*

This side view of the DSS&A ore dock illustrates the type of concrete construction and the position of the loading chutes. *Patrick C. Dorin*

This photo by Jim Scribbins shows DSS&A steam power shoving a train over the wooden section of the approach to the Marquette ore dock.

The 9659 (9525 – 9674) was part of the slanted end group of 50-ton ore cars operated by the DSS&A. This 1966 photo at the Marquette ore yard shows that this equipment still operated on arch-bar trucks. *Patrick C. Dorin*

DSS&A 9061 (9000 to 9399) was similar to the C&NW 50-ton ore cars. Note the side wheels for opening and closing the hopper doors. *Patrick C. Dorin*

No. 9088 did not have full sides, such as the 9061 illustrated previously. This group of cars was built in 1913 by American Car and Foundry. *Patrick C. Dorin*

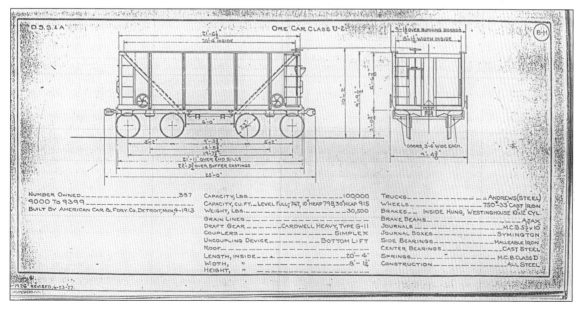

DSS&A Class U-2 ore car diagram, 9000 – 9399 series. *Soo Line diagram*

The Summers ore car No. 9609 literally was part of three different series. In this case, the 9609 was part of the 9525 to 9632 group. The cars were purchased from the Duluth, Missabe and Northern Railway. *Patrick C. Dorin*

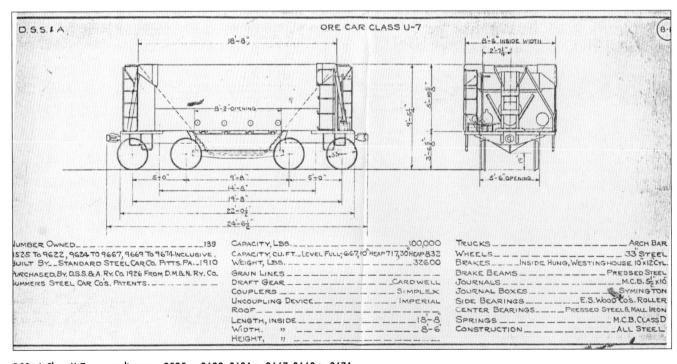

DSS&A Class U-7 ore car diagram, 9525 to 9622, 9624 to 9667, 9669 to 9674.

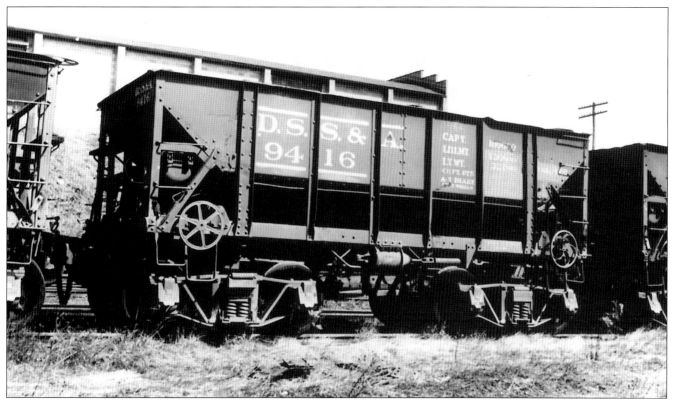

The 9416 was a former Duluth, Missabe and Northern Railway ore car. These were an interesting group of tapered side cars in the 50-ton capacity range. As can be observed, the cars rode on arch-bar trucks and had side wheels for opening and closing the hopper doors. *Patrick C. Dorin Collection*

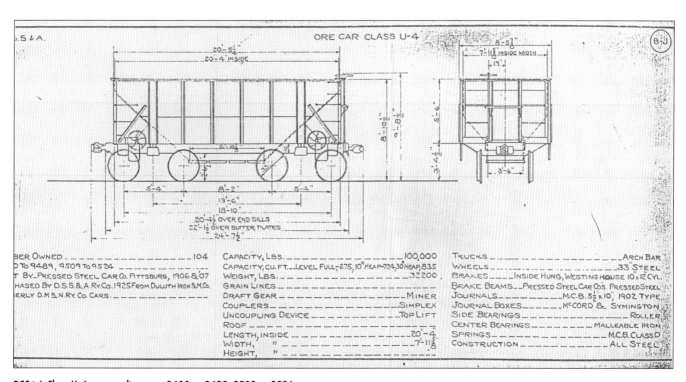

DSS&A Class U-4 ore car diagram, 9400 to 9489, 9509 to 9524.

CHAPTER 7
THE MILWAUKEE ROAD

The Milwaukee Road was a key player in the iron ore traffic of the Upper Peninsula of Michigan for many years. The company served the Menominee Range west of Escanaba since 1887. At the beginning of its ore hauling history, the Milwaukee Road operated their ore trains to Pembine, and then forwarded over the Soo Line Railroad to Gladstone, Michigan. The Soo owned and operated one ore dock at Gladstone, which was utilized by the Milwaukee Road shipments of iron ore. This operation continued until about 1901 when the Milwaukee Road began operations at Escanaba. Since the Milwaukee Road did not own a railroad line to the lake port, the company obtained trackage rights over the Escanaba and Lake Superior Railroad between Channing and Escanaba, a distance of 59.5 miles.

The Milwaukee Road operated over the E&LS until 1934 when an ore pooling agreement was reached with the C&NW. The pooling agreement continued until 1980 when the Milwaukee Road sold their railroad lines north of Green Bay, Wisconsin, to the Escanaba and Lake Superior Railroad. It is interesting to note that the E&LS played a role in the Milwaukee Road's ore operations from 1901 until 1934, and then picked up the ball again in 1980.

The Escanaba Ore Docks

The Milwaukee Road constructed their first ore dock and ore yard in Escanaba in 1901. In 1906, the company constructed their second ore dock. Both docks contained 240 pockets, 120 on each side, and were 1,440 feet long, pocket-to-pocket length.

The Milwaukee Road ore docks remained in operation until 1934 when the railroad began a pooling agreement with the Chicago and North Western Railway. From that time on, the Milwaukee Road ore traffic from both the Menominee and Marquette Ranges operated in conjunction with the C&NW. Milwaukee Road power, ore cars and cabooses operated to and from Escanaba over the C&NW. Thus, Milwaukee Road steam and later diesel power, as well as the ore cars were part of the picture on the C&NW docks in Escanaba.

The Modern Ore Car Fleet

The Milwaukee Road operated a fleet of wooden ore cars until they modernized the fleet with three orders for 800 new ore cars from Pressed Steel Car Company in 1928, 1929 and 1930. The cars were the only rectangular side ore cars to be operated on the Michigan ore lines. It is interesting to note that the Model Die Casting (Roundhouse) HO gauge rectangular side ore car is based on the Milwaukee Road prototype.

The new ore cars were numbered 75001 to 76599, odd numbers only. Over the years they carried several different lettering schemes, and of course, were always mixed in with C&NW ore cars.

During the 1960s when the iron ore pellets started to become the primary ore traffic, which require a large cubic space, the Milwaukee Road rebuilt 350 ore cars with 18-inch extensions. The cars were renumbered 76650 to 76999, both odd and even numbers. During the 1960s and '70s, the Milwaukee Road still operated 444 ore cars without extensions.

As a side note, sometimes Lake Superior and Ishpeming Railroad ore cars could be observed mixed in with C&NW and Milwaukee Road ore cars. Milwaukee Road ore cars were also observed in operation on the Soo Line in the Upper Peninsula, quite likely for rock service. The Milwaukee Road cars were often assigned to rock and ballast service in Wisconsin. Indeed it was interesting to see the ore cars in ballast service on the Northern Pacific, and mixed with NP ore cars, between Duluth and the Twin Cities.

Milwaukee Road ore cars also operated in coal train service in southern Indiana on the subsidiary Chicago, Terra Haute and Southeastern, especially during the winter season. Part of the fleet carried the reporting marks CTH&SE, or later on, simply CTSE.

It should be mentioned that the Milwaukee Road did, from time to time, interchange ore with the former Duluth, South Shore and Atlantic Railway at Champion, Michigan. Thus Milwaukee Road ore cars were observed from time to time in DSS&A trains.

The Milwaukee Road ore cars can be easily modeled using the Model Die Castings models mentioned above. They were colorful cars and the models bring back many memories of a neat operation. The cars were 24 feet long, coupled length; and 21 feet, 5 1/4 inches long between strikers, 9 feet, 5 inches wide, and 10 feet, 6 1/2 inches high.

Roster Summary

Car Numbers	Reporting Marks	Remarks
75001 to 75657	CTSE or CTH&SE	Odd numbers only
75659 to 76223	MILW	Odd numbers only
76225 to 76599	CTSE or CTH&SE	Odd numbers only

Cars with Extensions (Milwaukee Road Reporting Marks)

76650 to 76999   Rebuilt with 18-inch extensions with a height of 12 feet, 1 inch.

Final Group of Cars Without Extensions with MILW reporting marks

75001 to 76599   Odd numbers

This diagram illustrates the location of the two Milwaukee Road ore docks in Escanaba prior to the pooling arrangement with the Chicago and North Western Railway. The ore docks were of the same type of wood construction as for the C&NW docks to the right, as well as other wooden ore docks on Lake Superior. Escanaba is the last of what was once three shipping ports on Lake Michigan, the others being Gladstone and St. Ignace. *Milwaukee Road, drawn Oct. 1931*

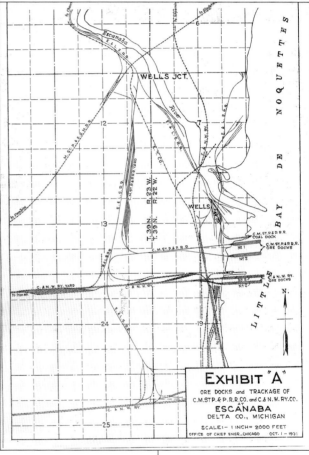

The data for this historical photo of these wooden ore docks at Escanaba is not complete and it is not known which railroad owned and operated this set of ore docks. It appears that they could be part of the original C&NW docks. However, the photo gives one a view of what the pair of Milwaukee Road ore docks could have looked like many decades ago. *Superior View / viewsofthepast.com*

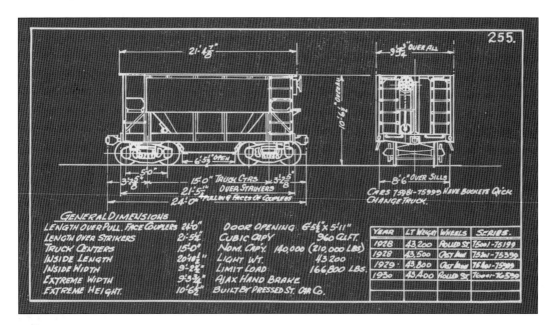

255.

21'-4 7/8"
9 5/4" OVER ALL

15'-0" TRUCK CTRS
6'-5 1/2" OPEN
21'-5 1/4" OVER STRIKERS
24'-0" PULLING FACES OF COUPLERS

8'-6" OVER SILLS

CARS 75981-75999 HAVE BUCKEYE QUICK CHANGE TRUCK.

GENERAL DIMENSIONS

LENGTH OVER PULL FACE COUPLERS 24'-0"
LENGTH OVER STRIKERS 21'-5 1/4"
TRUCK CENTERS 15'-0"
INSIDE LENGTH 20'-10 1/2"
INSIDE WIDTH 9'-2 1/2"
EXTREME WIDTH 9'-5 3/4"
EXTREME HEIGHT 10'-6 1/2"

DOOR OPENING 6'-5 1/2" x 5'-11"
CUBIC CAP'Y 960 CU.FT.
NOM. CAP'Y 140,000 (210,000 LBS)
LIGHT WT. 43,200
LIMIT LOAD 166,800 LBS.
AJAX HAND BRAKE
BUILT BY PRESSED ST. CAR CO.

YEAR	LT WEIGHT	WHEELS	SERIES
1928	43,200	ROLLED ST	75001-75199
1928	43,500	CAST IRON	75201-75399
1929	43,800	CAST IRON	75401-75999
1930	43,400	ROLLED ST	76001-76539

This diagram illustrates the dimensions of the Milwaukee Road and the Chicago, Terra Haute and Southeastern Railroad ore cars. The Milwaukee Road design was the only one of its kind on all of the ore lines. As a side note, the Pere Marquette and Chesapeake and Ohio railroads also owned a small fleet of such equipment for coal service for the car ferry operations on Lake Michigan. *Milwaukee Road diagram*

The Milwaukee Road repainted many of its ore cars with the larger lettering "Milwaukee Road." This photo of cars 76441 and 75135 show this scheme. *Patrick C. Dorin*

The last lettering design by the Milwaukee Road included the company insignia, such as illustrated on car 76545 in this photo at the Escanaba ore yard. It is interesting to note that Model Die Casting selected the Milwaukee Road ore car for its HO gauge model. *Patrick C. Dorin*

When the Milwaukee Road added 18-inch extensions to part of the fleet, the cars were renumbered 76650 to 76999, odd and even, such as the 76784.

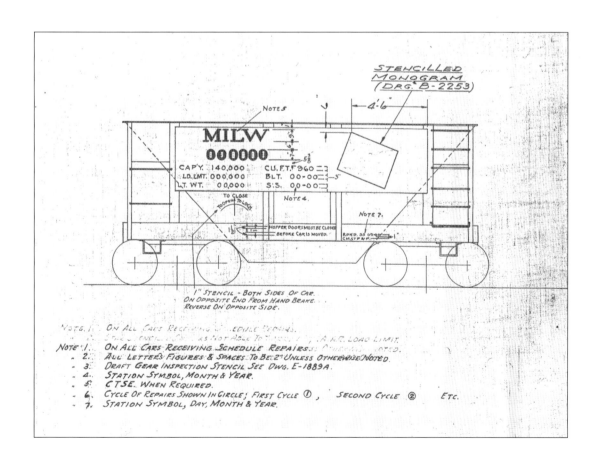

CHAPTER 8
THE CHICAGO AND NORTH WESTERN RAILWAY

The Chicago and North Western, like one of its team railroads the DM&IR, served two ports: Escanaba, Michigan, on Lake Michigan, and Ashland, Wisconsin, on Lake Superior. The railroad served three iron ranges in Michigan and also handled pellets from Minorca on the Mesabi Range during the winter seasons since the 1980s.

The C&NW, through the Peninsula Railroad Company began handling iron ore in the spring of 1864. The first ore was shipped through a Merchants Dock in Escanaba from the Jackson Mine at Negaunee, Michigan, on the Marquette Range. The C&NW began handling ore from Gogebic Range to Ashland in 1885. The company operated a wide variety of ore docks at the two ports including the current low-level ore dock in Escanaba, which as of 2004 is now part of the Canadian National Railway System.

The Ore Dock Systems

Escanaba

The C&NW built and rebuilt several ore docks at Escanaba, which was, for the most part, the only iron ore shipping port on Lake Michigan. (For a while, the Soo Line did have an ore dock at Gladstone, Escanaba's next-door neighbor on Little Bay de Noc.)

The Escanaba dock system is as follows:

Dock No. 1

The first ore dock replaced the Merchants Dock in 1872. It was 1,008 feet long and 37 feet high with 168 pockets. The ore dock soon proved to be too small, and it was rebuilt in 1889 with an extension to 1,104 feet and 48 feet, 6 inches high with 184 pockets. The rebuilt dock had a capacity of 24,104 tons. The dock was eventually dismantled in 1912.

Dock No. 2

The second dock joined No. 1 in 1881. It was 1,152 feet long but only 39 feet, 6 inches high. The dock was constructed with 192 pockets for a 20,928-ton storage capacity. The life span of the ore dock was 16 years as it was dismantled in 1897.

Dock No. 3

The No. 3 was actually constructed about the same time as the No. 2 and was 1,200 feet long and 39 feet, 6 inches high. The dock contained 200 pockets for a 20,000-ton storage capacity. It was rebuilt in 1895 with an extension to 1,356 feet long by 52 feet, 8 inches high including 226 pockets for a storage capacity of 30,284 tons. The No. 3 continued in operation until destroyed by fire during the fall of 1924.

Dock No. 4

This particular ore dock was completed in 1888. It was 1,500 feet long by 48 feet high with 250 pockets. The total tonnage capacity was 32,750 tons. The dock was actually destroyed by fire in late 1897, but was reconstructed in 1898 at 1,500 feet long and 59 feet high. The new dock contained 250 pockets with the same tonnage capacity even though the dock was 11 feet higher. Dock No. 4 was destroyed by the same fire that took down No. 3 in 1924.

Dock No. 5

No. 5 began the new era of much higher docks but at first was only 53 feet high and 1,392 feet long with 232 pockets and 43,152-ton storage capacity. The important fact about this ore dock was that it was rebuilt in 1909–1910 with a length of 2,220 feet and height of 71 feet. The newly constructed dock contained 370 pockets and 120,250-ton storage capacity. The dock continued in operation until after 1946 and was dismantled around 1960.

Dock No. 6

The last timber ore dock built on Lake Michigan was constructed in 1903. The new dock was 1,920 feet long with an 80,000-ton storage capacity. The dock was 70 feet high and contained 320 pockets. The ore dock was rebuilt in 1924 and continued in operation until 1969.

The Low Level Ore Dock

The new low level, 1,900-foot steel and concrete ore dock was built on the foundation of the No. 6 ore dock. It is equipped with a traveling ship loader with a pivoting boom for loading vessels of all sizes including the huge ore carriers with the 105-foot beam.

Time Periods of the Escanaba Docks

Dock Number	Dates in Operation
1	1872 to 1911
2	1881 to 1897
3	1880 to 1924
4	1888 to 1924
5	1891 to 1947 (Est.)
6	1903 to 1969
Low Level	1970 to Present

As one can see from the data, the C&NW once had as many as five docks in operation during the period 1891 to 1897. The iron ore port at Escanaba is still in full operation although with a different railroad than the Chicago & North Western System.

Ashland

The C&NW handled ore to Ashland for transloading to lake carriers from the year 1885 through 1962, the last season of shipping for the railroad. The original railroad to Ashland was the Milwaukee, Lake Shore and Western Railway. The line to Ashland was completed in 1885 and the company also began construction of the first No. 1 ore dock.

The C&NW took over the operation of the MLS&W in 1893 and rebuilt both the No. 1 and 2 extensively. Eventually a third ore dock was constructed for a total of three C&NW ore docks located in the east end of Ashland, which were numbered 1, 2, and 3. All three docks were in operation through 1936.

Dock No. 1

The first ore dock was 1,400 feet long, 46 feet high and only 40 feet high. The tonnage capacity was 26,000 tons in 234 pockets. No. 1 was rebuilt in 1916, possibly with a length of 1,740 feet. It was destroyed by fire and dismantled in 1936.

Dock No. 2

A second ore dock had been constructed in 1888 to the same specifications as the No. 1. However, the dock was eventually rebuilt with a length of 2,040 feet, 72 feet high and 340 pockets. There are some conflicting statistics regarding the length of the No. 2. An article in the *Skillings' Mining Review*, May 6, 1950, issue indicates the dock was 1,668 feet long with 278 pockets and 55,600-ton capacity. However, photographs seem to indicate that the No. 2 and 3 were the same length. The dock remained in operation through 1948. At that time, the C&NW retired the dock and leased 60 pockets on the Soo Line ore dock with night shift switching assignments only. No. 2 was dismantled beginning in 1950.

Dock No. 3

No. 3 was reconstructed in 1921 and was 2,040 feet long, 73 feet, 5 1/2 inches high and 51 feet, 6 inches wide, with 340 pockets for a total storage capacity of 85,000 tons. The ore dock continued in operation through the 1956 season. At that point the ore dock was scheduled for rebuilding. However a decision was made in January 1957 to halt the reconstruction and the C&NW began operating over the Soo Line ore dock in Ashland. This operation continued until 1962.

Thus at one time the C&NW had three docks operating at the same time in Ashland. The ore docks were fed by the ore yard on the east side of the city. When the C&NW dock operations ceased, various road-switchers were used to push the cuts of ore cars over the main line to the Soo Line ore dock approach. Prior to the Soo Line dock operations, the C&NW operated Alco and EMD switch engines. With the C&NW operating on the Soo Line dock throughout all three shifts, it was quite a delight to hear and see the shoves and pulls on the dock, which became quite frequent. There would be a Soo Line shove, and then the C&NW would be running up the ore dock too. It was not unusual to see sets of both Soo Line and C&NW power on the Soo ore dock. See the chapter on the Soo Line for more information about the company's dock in Ashland.

The Ore Car Fleet

The C&NW's ore car fleet was a mixture of both 50- and 70-ton ore cars from the 1920s through to the 1960s, and even beyond. The company's 50-ton ore cars were eventually replaced by a fleet of 50-ton cars purchased from the Duluth, Missabe and Iron Range Railway. Many of the 70-ton cars received extensions for iron ore pellet service, and the company purchased a number of such cars from the Lake Superior and Ishpeming Railroad.

The C&NW also purchased some 70-ton ore cars from the DM&IR, but also leased quite a number from both the DM&IR and the Bessemer and Lake Erie. These cars received C&NW reporting marks, but in some cases with the B&LE cars, the cars retained the Bessemer insignia.

Finally, one of the last major events with the C&NW took place when the railroad rebuilt a fleet of their 70-ton ore cars and painted them with a green color scheme. The cars retained their numbers but with an "R" added, indicating "rebuilt" equipment.

From the 1920s through to the 1960s, the C&NW's 50-ton ore car fleet could be divided into two groups. One had a 9-foot wide extreme width, while the other cars, that had the same appearance, had sides that sloped inward. This equipment was 8 feet, 11 inches wide, but were 7 feet, 9 7/8 inches wide at the top of the car. Most of the 50-ton cars were 22 feet, 6 inches long between strikers and 10 feet tall. (This is part of the fleet replaced by ex-DM&IR 50-ton cars later.)

50-ton Ore Car Roster – 1950s (Odd numbers only)
Equipment with the 9' width and 10' feet high

100001 to 101999
110001 to 111499

Equipment with the inward slopes with 8-feet, 11-inch width and 7 feet, 9 7/8 inches at the top.

111501 to 112499	10 feet high
112501 to 113499	9 feet, 9 inches high
120001 to 121599	9 feet, 9 inches high

70-ton Ore Car Roster – During the late 1950s
  The 70-ton ore cars were 24 feet long, coupled length with a 21-foot, 7-inch length over strikers. The cars were 10 feet, 7 inches tall and 9 feet, 4 inches wide. There was one series, 121601 to 122399, that was 10 feet, 8 inches tall.

2261 to 3010 (Odd and Even Numbers)
  This equipment was purchased in 1955 and they were the last new ore cars of the Lake Superior design purchased by the C&NW.

Following Odd Numbers Only:
113501 to 114499
118601 to 119099
119101 to 119999
121601 to 122399
122401 to 122699

Total number of ore cars for the mid to late 1950s was 4014 cars.

Ore Car Roster During the Late 1960s
During this period of time, the C&NW replaced many, if not all, of their original 50-ton ore cars with equipment from the DM&IR. Note the differences in dimensions.

50-ton Cars

110000 – 110999	24' 8" long coupler length, 9' 3" wide and 9' 7" high	171
111000 – 111999	same dimensions	574
		Purchased from the DM&IR

70 – 77-ton Cars

2261 - 3010	Without extensions	225
112000 - 112111	With extensions	106
112112 – 112511	With extensions	304
113501 – 114499	Without extensions, odd numbers	312
118601 – 119099	With extensions, odd numbers	244
119101 – 119999	Without extensions,	252
120000 – 120088	Without extensions	85
121601 – 122399	Without extensions, odd numbers	320
122401 – 122699	With extensions, odd numbers	145
122700 – 123040	With extensions,	340

Total number of ore cars		3173

Ore Car Roster During the Mid-1970s

No. Series	Remarks	No. Cars
2261 to 3010	77 tons. Did not receive extensions	214
118601 – 119099	77 tons with extensions (12 feet, 1-inch high) odd numbers only	218
120000 – 120088	77 tons without extensions	19
121001 – 121160	70 tons, leased from the DM&IR	61
121161 – 121204	70 tons, 27 feet, 2 inches long coupler length Leased from the Bessemer and Lake Erie	41
121601 – 122399	77 tons, odd numbers	5
122401 – 122699	77 tons, odd numbers, with extensions	134
122700 – 123040	77 tons, extensions,	315
Total Number of Cars		1221

Final Word on the C&NW ore cars

The C&NW owned a group of 77 ore cars that were not part of the Lake Superior design. These were 35-foot, 11-inch long cars with 100-ton capacity that were operated for the Black River Falls mine and pellet plant in central Wisconsin, number series 110500 – 110606.

The railroad also purchased an additional five hundred 77-ton capacity ore cars from the DM&IR, and numbered them in 810000 series.

The final group in 1995 is as follows:

Number Series	Quantity	Remarks
2261 – 3010	103	No extensions
112000 – 112611	434	Extensions
113501 – 114499	71	Odd numbers
118801 – 119099	186	Extensions and odd numbers
122401 – 122699	122	Extensions and odd numbers
122700 – 123040	110	Extensions
810000 – 810499	500	No extensions, ex-DM&IR
Total	1526	

The C&NW was purchased by the Union Pacific in the mid-1990s, and later the routes were purchased by the Wisconsin Central with new ore car reporting marks: SSAM.

The C&NW once operated three timber ore docks at Ashland, Wisconsin. By 1949, the number had been reduced to one, and the C&NW began moving some of its Gogebic Range ore traffic over the Soo Line dock at Ashland; and also to the Escanaba ore docks. This is the final dock No. 3, which has an Alco S-2 switch engine coupling up to a string of empty ore cars to be returned to the ore yard for assembly into a train for Ironwood and the Gogebic Range. *1954, Patrick C. Dorin Collection*

This view shows the C&NW wooden ore docks at Escanaba. Note the machinery on the side of the deck, which lower the chutes into an ore vessel for loading. The ore cars to the right are the 50-ton variety operated by the C&NW well into the 1960s — and even later. The C&NW ore docks had wooden trestles for the approach to the ore docks. *C&NW Photo, Patrick C. Dorin Collection*

The C&NW's last ore dock was the low level, conveyor belt system with a traveling ship loader, constructed in 1969. The loaded cars, from that time on, went through a car dumper with the raw iron ore or iron ore pellets handled by a conveyor system to a stockpile to wait for loading. However, in some cases, the pellets went directly from the car dumper to the ore dock for immediate ship loading. *Patrick C. Dorin*

These two photos show the entry and the exit to the Escanaba car dumper. When the cars were emptied, three cars at a time rolled out of the dumper and back to the ore yard. *1996, Patrick C. Dorin*

C&NW 50-ton ore cars, such as No. 110475 (Series 110001 – 111499, odd numbers), were a major part of the company fleet for many years. Until the 1950s, only 50-ton cars were in operation for the Gogebic Range – Ashland ore service, where they were mixed with Soo Line ore cars. They were also part of both the Marquette and Menominee Range operations to Escanaba, and were mixed with the C&NW and Milwaukee Road 70-ton ore cars. Compare this photo to the DSS&A 9061 on page 65. *Chicago and North Western Historical Society Archives*

Hidden to the right, 50-ton car 120737 illustrates the lettering after rebuilding at Clinton in 1958. *Robert C. Anderson*

The 70-ton cars were the tapered side variety, many of which were built by either Pullman Standard, or Bethlehem Steel. C&NW 119269 (Series 119101 to 119999, odd numbers) was built in April 1942 and first served on the Menominee and Marquette iron ranges. *Chicago and North Western Historical Society Archives*

This is a side view of 119909, which was built in July 1941. *Chicago and North Western Historical Society Archives*

These two photos of the 70-ton ore car 118923 (118601 to 119099, odd numbers) show two views of the group of cars built in 1953 by Bethlehem. This group's center braces at the A end of the car were indented a few inches, which set them slightly differently from many of the other 70-ton car groups. *Chicago and North Western Historical Society Archives*

As iron ore pellet traffic started, many of the ore lines rebuilt their ore cars with extensions, such as the C&NW's 118947 (118601 to 199099, odd numbers). The first groups of rebuilt cars, which were done at Clinton, Iowa, were painted in the boxcar red scheme (or similar to it) and received CNW reporting marks and the company insignia. Note the date 4-76 after the initials CLN, meaning it was worked on at Clinton in April 1976.

The last rebuilding cycle for the C&NW ore cars took place in the mid-1980s. The 122973 (from the 122700 to 123040 series) went through the Clinton shops in June 1985. The cars were repainted in an attractive green color scheme with yellow lettering and numbers. *Escanaba, 1985*

It is a cold January in 1973 at Norway, Michigan, on the Menominee Range. The first ore car, No. 121157, was part of a fleet of 60 cars (121001 to 121160, 70-ton capacity) that were leased from the Duluth, Missabe and Iron Range Railway. The cars retained the dark brown Missabe colors but with a boxcar red patch paint with the CNW reporting marks with the number below. The cars behind the 121157 were also ex-Missabe 50-ton capacity ore cars. Note the difference in the car sides as compared to the 110007 below. The tapered, smooth side car, Number 111240, is 9 feet, 7 inches tall. *Patrick C. Dorin*

The C&NW obtained over 700 50-ton ore cars from the DM&IR in the early to mid-1960s. The cars were smooth side with either a tapered side or a rectangular side. This car, No. 110007, was photographed on a foggy day in Escanaba in 1965 and illustrates a side view of this type of car. The car's shop date is listed as ESC 6-63, meaning its repainting, etc. was done in June 1963 at the Escanaba car shops. *Patrick C. Dorin*

This 3/4 view shows part of the end of the rectangular side cars with No. 110061 in this scene at Norway, Michigan, in 1973. *Patrick C. Dorin*

The tapered side car, No. 111565, is shown here with a snow-covered load of iron ore at Norway, Michigan. This group of equipment from the DM&IR replaced virtually all of the C&NW's 50-ton ore cars that had served the mining industry for many decades. *Patrick C. Dorin*

Another view of the leased fleet of 70-ton ore cars from the DM&IR that were repainted with a boxcar red patch and the CNW reporting marks, such as 121131 (121001 to 121160). This could be modeled with the Walther's DM&IR ore cars. *Joe Piersen*

The C&NW later acquired a fleet of 500 seventy-ton cars from the DM&IR. They received a patch paint job with the CNW reporting marks and the new number series 810000, such as the 810328 illustrated here. What is interesting is that the cars retained their high level air hoses as can be observed at both ends of the car, which is part of a consist of an all-rail ore train south of Superior, Wisconsin. *Patrick C. Dorin*

The 810000 series were not only used for ore service, but also rock and stone traffic as illustrated here with this photo of a trainload of stone by Joe Piersen.

DM&IR ore cars were common on the C&NW, either as leased equipment or for all-rail ore service. *Joe Piersen*

We will wrap up the chapter on the C&NW ore cars and dock with a photo of a leased ore car from the Bessemer and Lake Erie. Car No. 121170 (121161 to 121204) is shown here with its CNW reporting marks, but with the Bessemer insignia. Many of the cars did include a CNW insignia. This photo was taken in 1978 near Woodruff, Wisconsin, on the main line between Green Bay and Ashland. *Joe Piersen*

CHAPTER 9
THE LAKE SUPERIOR & ISHPEMING RAILROAD

The LS&I has been in operation since 1896 and is currently owned by Cleveland Cliffs. The railroad first constructed a wooden ore dock in Marquette in the mid-1890s. It was replaced by a new concrete ore dock in 1912 plus an expanded ore classification yard at the north end of Marquette. The ore dock area plus an incredibly beautiful park is known as Presque Isle.

The LS&I Ore Dock System

The LS&I No. 2 dock was constructed 1,200 feet long with 200 pockets, 100 on each side. Each pocket can handle 250 tons with a total ore dock capacity of 50,000 tons.

The ore dock is 75 feet high and 54 feet wide. Each of the 4 tracks can handle 50 ore cars at a time.

One interesting aspect of the ore dock is how the local electric generating plant built a coal receiver next to the ore facility. Ore boats loaded with coal can sail in, tie up at the ore dock, and unload the coal load with the ship's self-unloading conveyor system.

The coal is then transported by a conveyor system to the power plant's storage area.

Much, if not all, of the coal, is transported from Superior's coal loading system for movement to Marquette. As a side bar note: If the former Northern Pacific and Duluth South Shore & Atlantic Railroad tracks were still between Superior and Ashland and connecting with the remaining tracks at Nestoria, the coal traffic could move by rail all the way from the Powder River Basin to Marquette.

The LS&I once proposed building a new low-level ore dock for handling iron ore pellets at Rapid River, Michigan, on Little Bay de Noc on Lake Michigan. Rapid River is located to the east of Gladstone and Escanaba. The railroad also requested trackage rights on the Soo Line Railroad from Eben Junction down to the main line junction at Rapid River. The LS&I connected with the Soo Line at Eben Junction.

As an another side bar note: The LS&I once handled Ford Company ore to Doty, Michigan, for a connection with the Manistique and Lake Superior Railroad for movement to Manistique and a car ferry movement to Frankfort, Michigan, for all rail movements to Detroit.

The LS&I Ore Car Fleet

The LS&I currently operates the widest variety of ore cars in North America. Historically during the 1950s, most of the LS&I fleet consisted of 50-ton ore cars. However, as the 1950s rolled on and by 1964, the LS&I had acquired over 900 of the 70-ton cars, very similar to the C&NW ore cars of the same design. Now 50 years later in 2006, the fleet consists of many of the original 50-ton ore cars plus the 70-ton cars and all have been rebuilt with extensions for handling iron ore pellets. The company also purchased 85- and 90-ton capacity 24-foot ore cars during the mid 1960s. The railroad owns two different sets of this equipment, which is illustrated with the wide variety of photos of the LS&I fleet in this chapter.

The first LS&I ore dock was built of wood and is illustrated here in this photo prior to 1912, when the concrete ore dock was built to replace it. A switch engine with a slope back tender is approaching the dock facility to pick up a group of empty ore cars to return to the yard. *Superior View / viewsofthepast.com*

Ore Car Roster Prior to 1957

Number Series	Capacity	Remarks
1 to 400	50 Tons	LOS: 22', W: 9' 5", H: 10'
401 to 440	40 Tons	LOS: 22', W: 8' 3", H: 10' 6"
441 to 490	40 Tons	LOS: 22', W: 8' 3", H: 10' 6"
491 to 740	50 Tons	LOS: 22', W: 8' 3", H: 10' 10"
741 to 840	50 Tons	LOS: 22', W: 9' 5", H: 10'
841 to 1040	50 Tons	LOS: 22', W: 8' 8", H: 10' 10"
1100 to 1189	50 Tons	LOS: 22', W: 9' 2", H: 9' 8"
1300 to 1399	50 Tons	LOS: 22', W: 8' 8", H: 10' 2"
1400 to 1899	50 Tons	LOS: 21' 5", W: 9' 1", H: 10'

By 1970, all of the cars numbered from 1 to 1399 had been retired and or scrapped.
Many of the rectangular side 50-ton ore cars, 1400 to 1899, were upgraded with extensions and new 65-ton capacities.

7000 to 7499   70 Tons Tapered side cars with 7000 to 7149 numbers are very close to the Model Die Casting tapered side HO gauge ore car. This number series was in service on the LS&I prior to 1957. During the late 1960s, ore cars 7000 to 7199 had not received extensions.

The 1960s to the 21st Century

7200 to 7899   70 Tons- Upgraded to 77-ton capacities plus the 18-inch extensions increased cubic capacity from 975 feet to 1215 feet.

8500 to 8599   89 Tons- This set of equipment, purchased in 1964, was 24 feet long coupled length, 10 feet, 2 inches wide, and 12 feet, 3 inches high. Built by Bethlehem Steel. It was a unique design for ore cars, and only the Green Bay and Western acquired similar equipment. This group was painted in a red scheme.

8000 to 8199   85 Tons- Purchased in 1965, this set of equipment was 24 feet long coupled length, 9 feet, 8 inches wide and 12 feet, 3 inches high.

The ore cars with number series 1400 to 1899 were still in service moving into the 21st Century. All had been rebuilt with extensions and were 11 feet, 10 inches high.

The LS&I purchased a number of ore cars from the Duluth, Missabe & Iron Range Railway, which they modified and narrowed for operation on the ore dock. The company has also purchased a number of ore cars from the Long Island Railroad. These cars were originally owned and operated by the Canadian National and the Northern Pacific.

Former DM&IR Ore Cars

9000 to 9299	77 Tons	Cars rebuilt and narrowed by at least
9600 to 9699	77 Tons	8 inches to fit on the LS&I ore dock.

Other DM&IR ore car number series included 9300 to 9499.

Note: With the exception of the 8500 series, and the group listed below, the LS&I ore cars were painted black with white lettering.

Former Canadian National and Northern Pacific Ore Cars
Purchased from the Long Island Railroad in 2001

9500 to 9599   77- or 82-ton capacity cars, depending upon the origin of the cars: CN at 82, the NP at 77. The CN can be spotted by the four ribs below the rectangular side, while the NP equipment has square upper corners.

The 1912 ore dock is very active as we move into the 21st century, and it has had several modifications and updates for effective operation over the many years. As this is being written in 2006, the dock is 94 years old. This view was taken from the park located to the north of the ore dock area. *2003, Patrick C. Dorin*

This view illustrates the type of construction design for the base and the structure of the ore dock. A steel bridge is part of the ore dock approach. Note the ore cars on top of the dock. *2003, Patrick C. Dorin*

Two LS&I General Electric engines have just about completed making a shove of 40 loaded ore cars onto the dock. The 1,200-foot facility can accommodate 50 cars on each of the four tracks on top. This photo also shows the type of approach for the dock. *2003, Patrick C. Dorin*

An interesting aspect about the LS&I ore dock is the coal receiver facility for the power plant located near the ore yard. Ships can bring in coal, tie up at the ore dock, and with the self unloader conveyor system, can empty the coal into the receiver unit located to the right of the ore dock. The coal then moves by a conveyor belt system to the power plant. The ships load the coal at Superior, Wisconsin, and transport it to Marquette for the electric power plant. After unloading the coal, the ship can take on a boatload of iron ore pellets from the Marquette Range. *2003, Patrick C. Dorin*

The ore yard is located on the north side of the ore dock approach. The yard at one time played a major role in the classification and mixing of the various iron ores for steel plant needs and steel specifications. As this is being written in 2006, the LS&I serves only two mines and pellet plants and handles two to four types of pellets for shipping through the ore dock. This is substantially less then the days when dozens of mines were operating on the Marquette Range. *Patrick C. Dorin*

For our last view of the LS&I ore dock, let's take a look at the top. To improve safety, the LS&I installed steel beams at the top of the pockets. The pellets could easily flow through the openings, and it prevented any person working on the dock from falling into the pocket. *Patrick C. Dorin*

The LS&I has the widest variety of ore cars in service in the Great Lakes Region as we move into the 21st century. This makes the railroad very interesting for modeling, and for how ore cars can function over the long run. Car No. 1443 is a former 50-ton ore car with extensions and a new load limit of close to 67 tons. *Eagle Mills, October 2003, Thomas A. Dorin*

LS&I No. 1632 is a similar rectangular side ore car with a new load limit of 62 tons. *Eagle Mills, October 2003, Thomas A. Dorin*

Car No. 1753 is still another example of a rebuilt 50-ton car. *Eagle Mills, October 2003, Thomas A. Dorin*

The number series continues into the 1800s, such as the 1882 which illustrates the "B" end of the car. Note the R to the lower left on the car. This indicates the car has been rebuilt. *Marquette, August 2003, Michael A. Dorin*

No. 8051 is a rebuilt ore car, which was originally built in the mid-1960s. This type of ore car has a capacity of 88 tons, and is one of the largest capacities of the 24-foot ore car varieties. *Marquette, 2003, Patrick C. Dorin*

Car No. 8045 is in the consist of an ore train arriving in the Marquette ore yard. *Patrick C. Dorin*

Car No. 8159 is part of the newest series of equipment built in the mid-1960s. Note that it is higher than the rebuilt 50-ton ore car with extensions to the right. *Patrick C. Dorin*

LS&I 8593 was part of the second last group of new ore cars purchased by the railroad in the early 1960s. The cars were rated at 85 tons and were painted in a red color scheme. The cars were the only red cars on the roster for many years, but that would change in the early 2000s, which will be covered later in this section of LS&I ore cars. *Marquette, 2003, Patrick C. Dorin*

The LS&I has purchased a variety of ore cars from the Duluth, Missabe and Iron Range Railway over the years. The 9378 is one example of such equipment receiving an extension and painted yellow. The cars were known as "Banana Tops." *Marquette, 2003, Patrick C. Dorin*

Ore car No. 9495 was rebuilt with extensions, but did not receive the yellow paint scheme. The cars are similar to the Walther's LS&I HO gauge ore car models with extensions. This view shows the "A" end of the car. *Patrick C. Dorin*

The latest group of ore cars to be acquired by the LS&I is the 9500 series, such as the 9505, which was purchased from the Long Island Railroad. The heritage of many of the cars goes back to the Canadian National Railway. Note the four ribs below the rectangular side (CN design) compared to only two ribs on other "Minnesota" type ore cars from the Duluth, Missabe and Iron Range Railway. *Patrick C. Dorin*

Car No. 9513 is part of the fleet which now carries the box car red paint scheme. Note the placement of the hand brake on the extension on the B end of the car in this photo. *Eagle Mills, 2003, Patrick C. Dorin*

Car No. 9697 is another example of the rectangular side ore cars purchased from the DM&IR. *Patrick C. Dorin*

One more look at the 8000 series, 85-ton cars built in the mid-1960s. The 8068 has been rebuilt for testing air-operated doors, and thus has a different lettering arrangement than can be observed on the 8040. Note the striping on the bottom section of the frame. These two photos also show the cars have been rebuilt with roller bearings. *Thomas A. Dorin*

The first group of 70-ton ore cars for the LS&I was the number series 7000 to 7149. The cars were later rebuilt with extensions, but retained their original lettering and number placements, such as 7091 illustrated here.

The LS&I obtained a fleet of DM&IR ore cars for natural ore haulage to the pellet plants near Eagle Mills. The cars were painted in the LS&I black scheme with the lettering and numbers placed at the upper left, and the capacity data located in the middle of the car between the two sets of horizontal rivets. Car 9471 is part of the 9300 to 9499 series. Walther's rectangular side ore car is a perfect match for this group.

CHAPTER 10

THE WISCONSIN CENTRAL
SAULT STE. MARIE BRIDGE COMPANY

This chapter on the Wisconsin Central ore dock and ore car fleet is the result of a merger and the selling of the former Chicago and North Western Railway main line from Green Bay to Ishpeming, Michigan. The Union Pacific absorbed the C&NW in 1994, but the C&NW had already split the railroad with part of the main lines south of Green Bay to a subsidiary of the Green Bay and Western. Thus it was only natural for the UP to sell the properties with the Wisconsin Central being the ultimate owner. This added still another chapter to the successful WC operations in Wisconsin and Michigan.

When the WC completed the purchase of the ex-C&NW/UP lines, the company's subsidiary, the Sault Ste. Marie Bridge Company, was given the operating responsibilities. In fact, as the 24-foot ore cars were rebuilt and/or repainted, the cars received SSAM reporting marks.

The low-level ore dock built by the C&NW in 1969 continued to serve the Marquette ore operations through Escanaba. (Refer to Chapter 8). Not only are the Marquette Range pellets moving through the dock, but the company also handles pellets from the Minorca mine and plant on the Mesabi Range. This is primarily a winter operation.

The only change that really took place with the ore dock operations was the construction of an additional car dumper for handling 100-ton coal hoppers for the Minorca pellets.

The Canadian National purchased the WC in 2001, which now adds still another chapter to the WC ore operations. Since the Illinois Central is also part of the CN System, IC motive power has been observed handling Minorca trains between Escanaba and the DM&IR connection at Steelton, Minnesota. The Canadian National has also purchased the DM&IR, and thus the CN has added still another chapter in its iron ore traffic history.

The Ore Car Fleet

The WC acquired the C&NW fleet of ore cars. For quite some time, many of the cars still carried the variety of C&NW colors (green, red and more), with the new SSAM reporting marks and a variety of repaint jobs. The WC repainted a fleet of cars with WC red paint schemes and the SSAM reporting marks. The SSAM car numbers ranged from the 2200s through the 3200s.

Green Bay and Western Ore Cars

The GB&W was not an iron ore hauler, however the railroad did purchase a small fleet of 24-foot, 85-ton ore cars virtually identical to the Lake Superior & Ishpeming red ore cars in operation on the Marquette Range. The GB&W cars were operated in a variety of stone and ballast traffic, and also handled limestone for the steel mills in Sault Ste. Marie, Ontario. The cars were numbered 150 to 174.

When the Wisconsin Central purchased the former C&NW/UP ore lines in upper Michigan, the company's subsidiary, the Sault Ste. Marie Bridge Company, took over the routes with the reporting marks SSAM. The former C&NW ore cars were gradually repainted with the new markings, such as the 2449 shown here. *Eagle Mills, Patrick C. Dorin*

An end view of SSAM 2766 shows the placement of the lettering on the end of the extensions. *Eagle Mills, Patrick C. Dorin*

The ore cars have taken a beating over the years with the limestone loads from the port of Escanaba to the mining facilities. The mining company operated a machine that rolled over the tops of the cars to empty out the limestone. This really beat up the extensions quite badly as can be observed on the top of the 2768. *Eagle Mills, 2003, Patrick C. Dorin*

The SSAM 2829, an ex-C&NW ore car, has been freshly painted and this gives one an idea of what the entire fleet could have looked like in a few years. *Escanaba, 2001, Michael A. Dorin*

SSAM 2675 is a former C&NW in the new paint scheme and lettering. The trucks have been reequipped with roller bearings. This style of car is virtually identical to the Model Die Casting HO gauge ore with the types of ribs and other details. Note the ex-C&NW ore car to the right, which had grooved ribs at each end of the car. *Patrick C. Dorin*

SSAM 2354 illustrates the rebuilt trucks and other details. The photo shows the A end of the car, of which the center posts are a few inches inside away from the end. Note the letter R on these photos, which indicates that the ore cars have been rebuilt. *Patrick C. Dorin*

SSAM No. 2498 illustrates the type of C&NW ore car with the grooved ribs at the ends of the car. *Patrick C. Dorin*

The SSAM 3215 is a rebuilt ex-Lake Superior and Ishpeming Railroad ore car, which had been sold to the C&NW. This car is in the red color scheme. *Patrick C. Dorin*

SSAM 2731 is also a former LS&I ore car, but has only had the former reporting marks and numbers painted out, and replaced with the SSAM and number. The car, at this time, retains its LS&I black color scheme. *Patrick C. Dorin*

SSAM 3100 illustrates the complete repainting of a former LS&I rebuilt ore car. *Escanaba, 2001, Patrick C. Dorin*

The Green Bay and Western Railroad owned and operated a fleet of ore cars that were identical to the LS&I 85-ton full side cars. The cars saw service on the WC lines after the WC purchased the GB&W. The string of cars in this photo are loaded with rock and are being switched at the Steelton Yard in Sault Ste. Marie, Ontario. *1998, Patrick C. Dorin*

GB&W ore car No. 160. Note the similarity between this car and the LS&I 8500 series equipment. *Patrick C. Dorin*

CHAPTER 11

THE ALGOMA CENTRAL RAILWAY

The Algoma Central Railway had two basic ore operations. Iron ore moved on an all-rail basis from Wawa, Ontario, to the steel mills at Sault Ste. Marie, while the lake traffic moved from Wawa to Michipicoten Harbour, Ontario. The AC ore dock was the furthest east on the north shore of Lake Superior.

The Ore Dock System

The ore dock was not owned or operated by the Algoma Central, but rather by Landfill Mining Limited. The ore dock was a conveyor belt system, which was capable of handling 2,000 tons per hour. The dock consisted of two such systems, and was capable of loading 4,000 tons per hour. The dock system included a ground storage area with a capacity of 500,000 tons.

The ore dock at Michipicoten was built in 1939 and replaced an earlier pocket type ore dock. However, the pocket type dock was quite different from the others that had been built on Lakes Superior and Michigan.

The Modern Ore Car Fleet

The Algoma Central replaced its earlier ore cars by the early 1970s. The new cars were 100-ton hopper cars with two different designs. In fact, they are among the largest ore cars to be operated in the Lake Superior Region.

The 8001 to 8100 group was a rounded side type of car. The cars were 43 feet, 7 inches long — coupler to coupler — with 2,200 cubic feet of capacity. The second group was rib side cars numbered 8201 to 8500. This group was 43 feet, 10 inches long with 2,100 cubic feet of capacity.

The second group has also been modeled by Wm. K Walthers, Inc. of Milwaukee and is available in HO gauge. Model railroaders could practically duplicate an Algoma Central Railway ore train with some GP9s painted in the AC scheme. The caboose would be a more difficult. However, there was one brass Canadian National caboose manufactured by Overland Models that was very similar to the Algoma Central car.

The AC ore cars have been transferred to the Wisconsin Central and have served in a variety of bulk traffic services. The original dark green cars have been repainted into a lighter grey color scheme. The cars were sent to the WC after the Wawa mine closed. At the current time (2006), there is no iron ore traffic on the AC. However, interestingly enough the ore cars still show up at Sault Ste. Marie. Some of the cars have served in all-rail movements from the Marquette Iron Range to Soo, Ontario.

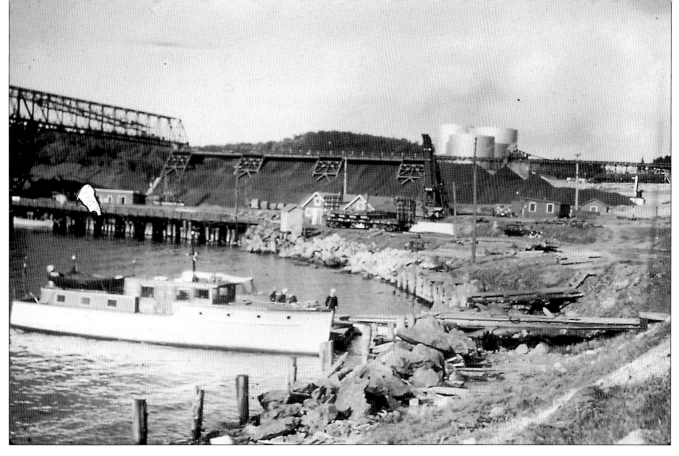

The Algoma Central operated one ore dock with a conveyor belt system at Michipicton Harbor. The ore dock handled a minimum amount of ore as time went on. The ores were shipped from the mine at Wawa directly to the Algoma Steel Company in Sault Ste. Marie, Ontario. *Algoma Central Railway Photos, Collection of the Author*

The Algoma Central owned and operated a larger size car for the ore service than was customary in the Lake Superior Region. The cars were in the 43 feet long category, and the AC operated the cars either to the ore dock or to Algoma Steel. The 8015 is shown here at Ishpeming, Michigan, after the Wisconsin Central purchased the Algoma Central. The cars were operated in a great deal of all-rail ore service. *Patrick C. Dorin*

The Algoma Central's rib side ore car was part of the fleet, and could be observed in not only iron ore service but also rock and stone traffic. *Patrick C. Dorin*

When the Wisconsin Central purchased the Algoma Central, a number of the ore cars were renumbered and given WC reporting marks, such as the WC 208029 shown here at Ishpeming, Michigan, in August 1998. *Patrick C. Dorin*

As time went on, many of the cars were repainted in a light grey color scheme with a red WC insignia and SSAM reporting marks, such as the 208344 illustrated here at Escanaba in 2001. *Patrick C. Dorin*

CHAPTER 12
THE CANADIAN NATIONAL RAILWAYS

The Canadian National Railways could be considered one of the most diverse ore haulers in the Great Lakes Region. Its first ore hauling operations began in 1944 with the opening of the Steep Rock Range, 140 miles west of Thunder Bay. However, the ore did not move to Port Arthur yet as the ore dock was under construction. At first, the ore moved west from Atikokan to Fort Francis. At that point, the trains turned south and rolled over the Duluth, Winnipeg and Pacific (a CN Subsidiary) to Superior, Wisconsin. The ore was interchanged with the Great Northern Railway and shipped over the Allouez docks. The CN's dock was completed in Port Arthur, now Thunder Bay, in 1945 with an extension in 1954.

The Canadian National also shipped pellets through the Valley Camp Coal Dock in Thunder Bay. The iron ore pellets came from the Bruce Lake area. Thus the railroad actually had two dock operations on the north shore of Lake Superior.

The second CN port for iron ore traffic was Picton, Ontario, on Lake Ontario. This ore shipping port was the furthest east of all Great Lakes ports and essentially outside of the primary Lake Superior Region. Picton is located 136 miles east of Toronto, which gives one an idea of just how far east this operation was located. The Picton dock was built by Bethlehem Steel for the movement of pellets from Marmora, a distance of 64 miles. The operation began in 1955.

The next ore hauling operation and port began operations in 1959. National Steel Company developed a mine and pelletizing plant at Moose Mountain, which is located north of Sudbury, Ontario. The ore was handled over the CN's Bala Subdivision to South Perry, and then over a 7.6-mile spur to Depot Harbor, which is located on the north shore of Lake Huron. The Moose Mountain operations were suspended in 1990.

Although the ore operations in Ontario were over for the most part, the CN is still in the ore hauling business with its purchase of the Wisconsin Central, the Sault Ste. Marie Bridge Company and the Duluth, Missabe and Iron Range Railroad. This chapter, however, covers only the CN ore operations in Canada.

The Canadian National Ore Dock Systems

Thunder Bay
The Canadian National built their 1,200-foot ore dock in two sessions. The first 600 feet was completed in 1945. The 600-foot extension was built in 1954. The ore dock was 82 feet, 6 inches high and 64 feet, 8 inches wide. 100 pockets were constructed with each 600-foot section for a total 200 pockets at 300 tons per pocket for a total storage capacity of 60,000 tons. At 1,200 feet, the ore dock could handle 50 ore cars per track. Ore operations on the original ore dock ended in the early 1980s with the Steep Rock area closing down.

The Valley Camp Coal Company dock was a conveyor system operation. The company began operations with Valley Camp when additional ore mines and pellet plants went into operation at Bruce Lake 253 miles northwest of Thunder Bay. This operation came to an end in 1990 when the Bruce Lake operations were shut down.

Picton, Ontario on Lake Ontario
The Picton ore dock was built in 1955 by Bethlehem Steel. It was a conveyor belt system with a dock 765 feet long and a 63,000-ton storage area. The storage area was 40 feet deep and about 800 feet long and 50 feet wide at the top. The bottom of the pit fed into a concrete conveyor tunnel. Loaded cars were dumped by moving them over a steel trestle with a single track over the pit. A single conveyor system could be extended out over the ore boats for loading. The dock had an approximate 2,000 tons per hour loading rate.

The standard 24-foot ore cars were not used for this operation. Instead, the CN assigned 100 hopper bottom "battleship" type gondolas for ore service to the Picton dock system.

Depot Harbor, Ontario
The Depot Harbor operation began in 1959 and was a conveyor belt system type of ore dock. The dock had a 300,000-ton storage area that was 800 feet long. The Depot Harbor operation ended in 1990. The Canadian National operated the 24-foot ore cars for the Depot Harbor dock.

The Canadian National Ore Car Fleet

62.5-ton Cars

Car Numbers

114100 to 114699	Rectangular side ore cars very similar to the Minnesota cars but 9 feet, 7 inches wide and 10 feet, 1-inch high. This group was built in 1944 and 1947 and composed the entire fleet of ore cars during the mid-1950s.
341000 to 341541	Renumbering system for the 62.5-ton cars without extensions.

82.5-ton Cars

122000 to 123079	Rectangular side ore cars built by National Steel in 1957.
343000 to 343085	Renumbering system for the 82.5-ton cars without extensions.

Rebuilt Cars with 21-inch Extensions

62.5-ton Cars

342117 to 342139	Cubic feet increased from 825 to 1,130. Total height with the extension was 11 feet, 10 inches.

82.5-ton Cars Increased to 85-ton Capacity

344000 to 344866	Cubic feet increased from 1,000 to 1,350. Total height with the extension was 11 feet, 11 inches.

All of the CN ore cars were built by National Steel Car. The cars received the renumbering and the new CN logo when rebuilt.

The Port Arthur ore dock was built in two stages, 600 feet at a time. The 1200-foot dock is the same length as the LS&I ore docks. *Patrick C. Dorin collection*

CN ore car No. 341153 was part of the original group of ore cars purchased by the Canadian National. After repainting and other repairs, the original 114000 series cars were renumbered to the 341000 group, which did not receive extensions. In many respects, this group with a 62.5-ton capacity is closer to Walther's HO gauge 70-ton ore car model than the 82.5-ton capacity cars. Two examples are the placement of rivets and the fact that the car has only two braces. The group was later re-listed at 68-ton capacity. *Thomas A. Dorin*

CN ore car 343052, from the renumbered 343000 series, is part of the 82.5-ton capacity fleet that did not receive extensions. *Thomas A. Dorin*

Car No. 341043 is another example of the 62.5-ton capacity fleet, but in this case the car has four braces and the rivet arrangement is identical to the later group of 82.5-ton capacity cars. Note the placement of the rivets at the center of the car. This was part of the group of cars purchased in 1946. *Patrick C. Dorin*

Canadian National ore car 343076, an 82.5-ton capacity car, illustrates the lettering on the cars when first built in 1957 but with the number change. The 82.5-ton capacity cars without extensions were renumbered from the original 122000 series to the 343000 series group. *Patrick C. Dorin*

Many of the 82.5-ton capacity cars were rebuilt with extensions and renumbered into the 344000 series, such as the 344137 illustrated here. Note that the brake wheel on the B end of the car was raised and placed on the extension. *Patrick C. Dorin*

CHAPTER 13

THE DULUTH, WINNIPEG AND PACIFIC RAILWAY

This is a brief chapter on the DW&P and its relationship to the ore mining industry. The DW&P never did own or operate any ore docks on Lake Superior, but it did handle iron ore. For a brief period of time during World War II, and until the Canadian National's ore dock was built in Port Arthur, now Thunder Bay, the DW&P handled iron ore from the CN at Fort Francis to the Great Northern in Superior, Wisconsin.

The next chapter of ore traffic on the DW&P involved a trackage rights agreement for the DM&IR to operate over the "Peg" to serve the Minorca Pellet plant for Inland Steel. The DW&P did own a small fleet of ore cars, which were rebuilt for rock and ballast service. The rebuilt ore cars were purchased second hand from the DM&IR, and were painted in the CN/DW&P's red colors with white lettering and numbers. This was the only fleet of ore cars ever to be owned by the DW&P. It is interesting to note that the DM&IR's rebuilt ballast cars were also sold to the EJ&E.

(Refer to Chapter 1)

Roster Summary

53311 to 53319   Ex-DM&IR with 14-inch extensions. Note: Refer to DM&IR diagram on page 34 and photo on page 33.

The DW&P acquired a small fleet of ore cars from the DM&IR. They had been rebuilt for ballast and rock service. Note the ballast hopper doors on the 53311 in this photo, which was taken at the new Pokegama Yard (south of Superior, Wisconsin) in June 1997. *Patrick C. Dorin*

CHAPTER 14

THE CANADIAN PACIFIC RAILWAY

The Canadian Pacific was one of the minor ore operations within the Lake Superior - Lake Huron area. The railroad handled an iron ore by-product from the processing of nickel-iron-copper-sulfide ores. The CP handled the ore from the International Nickel Company's smelter over an 80-mile route to the port at Little Current, Ontario, on Lake Huron.

The Ore Dock Facility

The Little Current dock was equipped with a bridge and seven-ton clam bucket for loading boats. The loading process was relatively slow with an approximate 1,500 tons per hour rate. The ore dock itself was 1,500 feet long with a ground storage capacity of 50,000 tons. The dock was built in 1915. Little Current is located on Manitoulin Island, just off the north shore of Lake Huron. CP's branch line to the port came off the Sault Ste. Marie - Sudbury main line at Mc Kerrow.

CP Ore Cars

The Canadian Pacific ore cars for the Little Current ore train traffic were gondola type cars equipped with five drop bottom doors on each side. The group from number series 376500 to 376846 had a capacity of 75 tons. One hundred of the cars were rebuilt with 18-inch extensions, which in turn provided an 81-ton capacity. The cars were longer than the 24-foot Lake Superior ore car fleet. The cars measured 31 feet, 2 and 5/8 inches inside the coupler faces. The cars were 9 feet, 4 and 1/8 inches tall prior to the 18-inch extension.

The Little Current service was the only iron ore traffic on the Canadian Pacific.

It turns out that CP tracks run through areas of various types of iron ore deposits that have yet to be set up for mining. One never knows which direction traffic levels can go, and it could be said perhaps some day the CP will be a major iron ore hauler.

The Canadian Pacific owned and operated a fleet of ore cars that were similar to the Lake Superior type of car, but were longer and with a larger cubic capacity. The four ore cars shown in this photo were sent from British Columbia for testing in the Sudbury, Ontario, area in 1978. This equipment was 29 feet, 8 inches long, coupler-to-coupler length compared to the 24-foot length for the Lake Superior cars. This set of four cars (377060, 377017, 377185 and 377246) illustrates the two types of lettering arrangements used on the ore cars during the 1960s and beyond. *Gordon Jomini*

CHAPTER 15

ERIE MINING COMPANY
LTV STEEL MINING COMPANY

Erie Mining Company built its railroad from Hoyt Lakes to Taconite Harbor starting in 1954 with completion in 1956. The railroad line extends for 74 miles to Lake Superior. The company railroad handled over two million tons of pellets to the dock in 1958. As time went on from the late 1950s through the year 2000, the annual pellet shipments were generally from six to eight million tons. The record year was 1973 with over 13.1 million tons. The final year of operation was 2001.

Taconite Harbor and the Ore Dock System

The ore dock itself is approximately 1,200 feet long with a storage capacity of 100,000 tons. The ore dock trackage is part of a loop for unloading the ore trains from Hoyt Lakes. As a train arrived at the dock, a special unloading system on the ore cars opened the hopper doors of the cars as it rolled over the dock. A special wheel system on each side of the ore cars connected with a rail system to open and close the doors during the train movement. In fact, the system could actually unload a complete train consisting of 96 to as many as 120 cars in about 15 to 30 minutes.

The dock was constructed with 25 pellet storage bins on 48-foot centers. Each bin is serviced with a retractable conveyor belt system for loading the ore vessels. Each bin can store up to 4,000 tons of pellets.

The ship loading conveyor belts are 42 inches wide and with a shuttle length of 91 feet can accommodate any type of ore vessel. The maximum reach beyond the side of the ore dock is 44 feet with a height of 37 feet above the water. The loading capacity of the belt systems for each bin is about 1,500 tons per hour. However, the actual loading time per bin can be somewhat longer depending upon how the loading process can be handled by a particular ship. A typical 1,000-foot boat will be loaded by 18 belts at Taconite Harbor. A 55,000-ton cargo (a usual load given the lake levels during the past few years) spread over 18 bins results in just over 3,000 tons coming out of the bin rather then all 4,000 tons stored there. At the 1,500 tons per hour rate, it takes two hours to load the boat at full speed on the belts. Docking, less than full speed belt, balancing, trimming and departure make up the 4 to 6 hour time period that normally occurs.

Although it was easiest for the Taconite Harbor ore dock to handle one product, it can handle more than one type of ore or pellets but not at the same time. Since 1987, the dock has also handled chips and red ore. The last of the red ore went through the dock in 1994.

Since the overall North American economy is expected to grow over the next twenty years of the 21st Century, with substantial increases in freight traffic for all transportation modes, the Taconite Harbor Ore Dock must be kept in mind for future work.

The Ore Car Fleet

Erie Mining Company originally purchased 389 pellet cars from Bethlehem Car Company in 1956. The original fleet was lettered for the Erie Mining Company and was numbered 3000 to 3388. The cars weighed approximately 60,500 pounds (plus or minus 200 pounds) and with an 85-ton capacity. The overall length inside the coupler faces is 37 feet, 8 inches.

It is interesting to note that when Erie Mining Company increased the plant production capacity from 7.5 million tons to 10.5 million tons of pellets in the mid-1960s, due to the increased efficiency of the "in-motion" pellet car dumping system, additional cars were not needed. The original number of the fleet was sufficient and no new cars were ordered until 1997.

LTV Steel Corporation absorbed the Erie Mining Company in 1986, and changed the name to LTV Steel Mining Company. Because of a derailment and a loss of a number of pellet cars, LTV purchased 96 new Difco 90 long-ton capacity ore cars in 1997. The new cars, numbered 3401 to 3496, carried the reporting marks LTVX.

At the present time, 2007, the former LTV plant is still idle. Cleveland Cliffs recently purchased the facilities, renamed the facility Cliffs-Erie, and renamed the rail line the Cliffs-Erie Railroad.

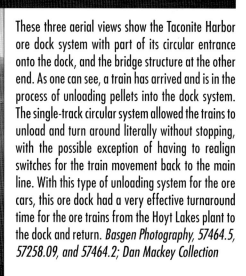

These three aerial views show the Taconite Harbor ore dock system with part of its circular entrance onto the dock, and the bridge structure at the other end. As one can see, a train has arrived and is in the process of unloading pellets into the dock system. The single-track circular system allowed the trains to unload and turn around literally without stopping, with the possible exception of having to realign switches for the train movement back to the main line. With this type of unloading system for the ore cars, this ore dock had a very effective turnaround time for the ore trains from the Hoyt Lakes plant to the dock and return. *Basgen Photography, 57464.5, 57258.09, and 57464.2; Dan Mackey Collection*

TACONITE HARBOR

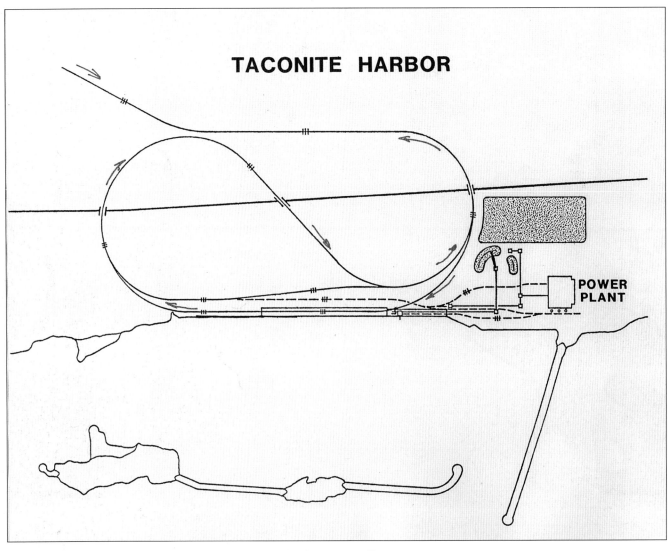

Map of the trackage approach to the ore dock and the adjacent facilities. *Doug Buell*

This view shows the Taconite Harbor ore dock's conveyor belt system for loading the ore vessels. *Basgen Photography, 65231-19, Dan Mackey Collection*

Five Erie Mining Company "F" units are arriving at the Taconite Harbor ore dock. Note the outbound track to the left. The Erie Mining Company eventually became part of LTV, with a change in color schemes and reporting marks for the equipment. *Basgen Photography, 65231.5, Dan Mackey Collection*

This side view of the former Erie, later LTV, ore car illustrates the rubber tire system used for the automatic, non-stop unloading process on the ore dock. With side rails on the dock connecting with the tires, the hopper doors could be opened and closed at the appropriate time for unloading the entire trainload into the ore dock. Car No. 042 is part of a consist departing Hoyt Lakes and is en route to Taconite Harbor during the summer of 1995. *Patrick C. Dorin*

LTV purchased a fleet of new ore cars to replace several that had been damaged in a derailment. The new cars were delivered in 1997 and carried the LTVX reporting marks as illustrated on car 3409 in this photo by Steve Ruce.

CHAPTER 16

RESERVE MINING COMPANY RAILROAD/ NORTHSHORE MINING COMPANY RAILROAD

The Reserve Mining Company began operations in 1956. It is the only railroad in North America to haul raw taconite ore to a plant located at a Lake Superior port, in this case at Silver Bay, Minnesota, approximately 50 miles northeast of Duluth. Reserve built a 47-mile railroad from Babbit, Minnesota, to Silver Bay along with an ore train yard on top of the hill overlooking Lake Superior. The ore train yard includes a car dumper that feeds the ore to the pelletizing plant on the lakeshore.

Reserve Mining was closed for a period of time in the 1990s, and has been reorganized as the Northshore Mining Company.

The Ore Dock System

The company built and eventually expanded a conveyor system type of ore dock with 10 silos. Each silo, or bin as they are called, can handle 5,000 tons of pellets. The ore dock capacity by itself is 50,000 tons. The pellet storage yard is located behind the dock, which is parallel to the lakeshore. Two conveyor systems load the ore carriers, and are capable of loading the 1,000-foot carriers. Ore carrier loading times are approximately 4 hours for 25,000-ton capacity ships, and 8 to 12 hours for the 1,000-foot carriers.

The Ore Car Fleet

The ore car fleet consists of 29 feet, 10-inch coupler-to-coupler length, flat bottom equipment. The cars are built for the rotary dump system at the Silver Bay ore train yard. The cars are switched for dumping in 26 car blocks. Each block takes approximately four hours for dumping including placement and switch moves.

As cars are purchased new or repainted, the cars are lettered NSMX.

The Roster

Number Series	Remarks
100 to 1104	Part of the original roster of Reserve Mining Co.
1150 to 1191	Newest group within the fleet

The Northshore Mining ore dock at Silver Bay is equipped with a conveyor belt system for loading the ore vessels. In this aerial view, one can see the conveyor extension system pouring pellets into a lake carrier. *Basgen Photography, 71404-7, Dan Mackey Collection*

An aerial view of the Silver Bay taconite processing plant, ore train yard and dock facilities. *Basgen Photography, 80536-8, Dan Mackey Collection*

The taconite ore trains arrive at the yard facility at Silver Bay. The ore is moved by a conveyor belt system to the plant for the pellet production. This view shows the Silver Bay Yard. *Patrick C. Dorin*

The loaded cars are moved through a car dumper for unloading. *Patrick C. Dorin*

Northshore Mining uses switch engines for moving the cars to the car dumper. Note that the ore cars are solid bottom cars, which means they must move through a rotary dumper for unloading. *Patrick C. Dorin*

The rotary car dumper mechanism. *Basgen Photography, 63377-4, Dan Mackey Collection*

Close up view of the Northshore Mining switch engine No. 1212. Note that the headlight has been elevated for better viewing during nighttime assignments at the Silver Bay Yard. *Patrick C. Dorin*

Motive power such as the 6048 are operated for over-the-road ore trains as well as some switching work from time to time. *2003, Silver Bay, Patrick C. Dorin*

The tailings are loaded into side-dump cars, such as No. 1660 illustrated here at Silver Bay. *Patrick C. Dorin*

When the taconite ore has been processed into the high-grade pellets, the material left over, known as tailings, is handled by a conveyor belt system to a loader at the yard facility in Silver Bay. Train consists of dump cars are moved through the tailings loader for transportation to a storage facility, known as the Dumping Ground, about six plus miles from Silver Bay. The loaded trains run to the area, unload the tailings and return to Silver Bay. *Patrick C. Dorin*

One of the older ore cars, No. 869, only shows its number as the reporting marks have been covered over by dust and other material. *2003, Patrick C. Dorin*

The newer ore cars are built to the same design as the original fleet in order to accommodate the cars in the dumping facility at Silver Bay. NSMX 1151 illustrates the black and yellow color scheme. The NSMX reporting marks indicate a private car line ownership meaning Northshore Mining. *Patrick C. Dorin*

NSMX No. 993 illustrates the placement of the hand brake and other equipment on the ends of this unique ore car design. *Patrick C. Dorin*

A loaded train has arrived and is now awaiting the switching moves for unloading. Once unloaded, the train will be reassembled and will travel back to Babbitt for another load of taconite ore. *Patrick C. Dorin*

CHAPTER 17

THE BESSEMER AND LAKE ERIE RAILROAD

The Bessemer and Lake Erie was, and is, an important ore hauler from Lake Erie to the Pittsburgh area steel mills. Although the railroad is not a "Lake Superior Iron Ore Railroad," the company did own and operate a fleet of ore cars. One set of the ore cars was very similar to the Lake Superior concept, but were somewhat longer. The second set of cars was actually purchased from the company's sister railroad, the DM&IR.

The first set of cars was purchased from Greenville Steel Car Company in 1952.

The cars were virtually an identical design of the Lake Superior cars. However, they had end sills and were 27 feet, 2 inches, coupler to coupler length and 10 feet, 9 inches high. The number series of the cars was 20000 to 20700.

Later the ore cars were rebuilt with extensions which gave them a height of 11 feet, 7 inches. The rebuilt cars were numbered from 20701 to 20890.

A number of the B&LE ore cars were sold to other railroads. One group was sold to the Chicago and North Western. For the most part, the cars were in rock service on the C&NW, but I have been told that they did sometimes see all-rail ore traffic.

Model Power Products has manufactured the B&LE ore cars in HO gauge.

The second set of ore cars came from the DM&IR. This was a group of cars that had been rebuilt by the DM&IR with the 9 and 3/4-inch extensions. The rebuilt cars for the B&LE were numbered 20900 to 20982. It turns out that this set of equipment has been manufactured by Walthers in HO gauge with the correct paint scheme and lettering.

Modelers could easily make up a B&LE ore train with the two types of ore cars that were available in the fantastic model railroad market.

As we roll into the 21st Century, most of the B&LE ore traffic is handled in 100-ton capacity coal hoppers. The B&LE is now part of the CN.

This is one of the final appearances of the B&LE ore cars. Although similar to the Lake Superior type of ore cars, the B&LE cars had extended ends and were longer than 24 feet. The B&LE did purchased a number of DM&IR rebuilt ore cars for taconite service. Walther's B&LE taconite ore cars are 100% correct for the B&LE purchase of the DM&IR equipment. This photo was taken by Richard Ganger when the research for this book began several years ago. *Patrick C. Dorin Collection*